FATHER
MEMORIES

FATHER MEMORIES

How to discover the unique, powerful, and lasting impact your father has on your adult life and relationships

RANDY L. CARLSON, M.A.

MOODY PRESS
CHICAGO

ISBN: 0-8024-2819-3

1 3 5 7 9 10 8 6 4 2

CONTENTS

FOREWORD

R andy Carlson and I are cohosts of the nationally syndicated
talk show "Parent Talk." When you work as closely as we do
you get to know each other well. We are both counselors; in
fact, we both went through the same graduate program. We have
two wives and seven kids between us. We deal with many people
behind closed doors. We see the hurts daily—the scars, if you will
—people whose memory banks are filled with nothing but ridicule, abuse, and memories of fathers and mothers they would
choose to forget, if that were possible.

First let me say that you will enjoy reading *Father Memories.* If
you've already read *Unlocking the Secrets of Your Childhood Memories* (Nashville: Thomas Nelson, 1989; New York: Simon & Schuster [Pocket Books], 1990), which Randy and I co-authored, you
already have a clear picture of how memories can affect your life,
the mate you choose, the type of parent you become, and the kind
of walk with God that you will have.

I believe most people think a father's main role at home is to
provide for his family's physical and material needs and to serve
as an authority figure. But Randy and I learned a long time ago that
fathers provide more than that. They leave an indelible imprint on
their children, particularly upon their daughters.

In *Father Memories* Randy demonstrates that your life has
been significantly and permanently affected by your father. He
may have been home a lot, or he may have spent most of his time

7

working. He may have been with your family all the years you were growing up, or he may have died or abandoned the family when you were quite young. Whatever role your dad took, the father memories you built over the years were the major blocks upon which your character, lifestyle, relationships, and choices were formed.

As Randy says, "Your father stamped his seal on your life, both genetically and psychologically. Father memories can't be shaken off, grown out of, or painted over. They can, however, be explored, comprehended, and incorporated internally in ways that lead to lasting change." That is what this book is designed to help you do.

A father memory is more than a look at the way things were when you were a child. It is a look into your personality today. The woman whose father memories include stepping into her father's footsteps in the deep snow is the same woman who enjoys challenges today and who believes that she can accomplish her goals. The man who remembers his dad's inviting him to open the front door and come outside to see the gift he had brought is the same man whose initiative and creativity has led him to found a ministry that has strengthened thousands of families.

Not all father memories are positive, however. No dad is perfect. But making your dad the scapegoat for your troubles will not lead to healing. As I tell people frequently, yes, life kicked you squarely in the teeth, but the point is, what are you going to do about it? Are you going to pick yourself up and get going, or are you going to let past events and memories emotionally handcuff you for years to come?

God can help you see your father as he really is, not just as your memories depict him, and He can help you forgive the mistakes your father may have made. Randy offers a unique prescription filled with real-life examples to help you find a path to emotional health.

As you journey through your father memories you will uncover family characteristics you would like to change and encouraging patterns that are worthy of imitation and reinforcement. You hold in your hands the opportunity to make lasting changes in the lifestyle you have learned and to build on the positive traits your parents established as they reared you. *Father Memories* can help you establish deeper, more fulfilling relationships, come to peace with your past, and find hope for your future.

Dr. Kevin Leman

ACKNOWLEDGMENTS
AND DEDICATION

The idea for this book came as an outgrowth of my first book, *Unlocking the Secrets of Your Childhood Memories* (coauthored with Kevin Leman). As a result of that book I have had the opportunity to travel across the country to lead seminars on the topic of early memories.

Everywhere I've gone people have wanted to talk about not simply their early memories but specifically their father memories. The more father memories I analyzed the more convinced I became that a book needed to be written that looked specifically at fathers and their impact on our memories and our lives.

I want to thank my co-workers at Family Life Radio and the radio program "Parent Talk" for their encouragement and patience during the times of heavy writing and editing.

I also want to thank my wife, Donna, and children, Evan, Andrea, and Derek, for their understanding when I disappeared into my office to write.

And what can I say about Kevin Leman? To him go profound thanks for his "hang in there" and "you can do it" encouragement.

I would also like to thank Rita Schweitz and Jim Bell for their untold help and direction.

To my mom: Thanks always for your unfailing support and love.

And, finally, to my dad: This book is for you. Without the foundation you laid in my life I don't know where I'd be today. I dedicate this book to you with a prayer that God will give you many more years of service. And thanks for the memories.

Part 1

Why Your Father Memories Matter

1

FATHER MEMORIES—
YOUR WINDOW TO THE WORLD

Fathers leave a lasting impression on the lives of their children. Picture fathers all around the world carving their initials into their family trees. Like a carving in the trunk of an oak, as time passes the impressions fathers make on their children grow deeper and wider. Depending upon how the tree grows, those impressions can either be ones of harmony or ones of distortion.

Some fathers skillfully carve beautiful messages of love, support, solid discipline, and acceptance into the personality core of their children. Others use words and actions that cut deeply and leave emotional scars. Time may heal the wound and dull the image, but the impression can never be completely erased. The size, shape, and extent of your father's imprint on your life may be large or may be small but it is undeniably there.

Your father's imprint upon you is best recognized in what you remember of your father's words and actions in relationship to you as a child. Think back to any moment or event of your childhood when you and your father were both present. That recollection is what I call a father memory.

Your father memories reveal how your father contributed to your perception of yourself, others, and life. Father memories are comparable to videotapes played repeatedly in your conscious and subconscious mind that in turn motivate your words and actions in the present.

Think back over the major events of your childhood. If your father was not a part of your life, think about the male authority figure who had the most significant impact on you as a child. Perhaps a grandfather, uncle, stepfather, older brother, or even a teacher or neighbor became your father figure. Check the introductory statements below that fit your father memories:

_____ "I remember tender, touching, and secure moments."

_____ "I remember sitting on Dad's lap, hugging, and other physical signs of affection."

_____ "I remember doing things with my dad and being happy."

_____ "I recall Dad being distant or absent. We had little contact."

_____ "I recall feelings of fear and anxiety when my father was around—I never knew what to expect."

_____ "I don't remember much at all about my father."

_____ "My dad died (or left) when I was a child. I only have stories that others have told me about him."

_____ "When I remember what it was like to be my father's child, I recall feelings of . . ."

> _____ tenderness
> _____ insignificance
> _____ security
> _____ shame
> _____ affirmation
> _____ rejection
> _____ belonging

As you think about your life before you were ten, what comes to mind? The words you use and the emotions you attach to each father memory are extremely important. Some memories are sharp and clear, others vague and confusing, but all are important and influence the values, attitudes, and goals woven into the fabric of your life. The dark and light threads that appear in your early childhood memories are still on the loom today.

Your father memories reveal your basic personality, your style of relating to others, po-

tential conflicts in relationships, and the life
themes that determine your view of life.

If you are a woman and are able to relate well to men, you'll
find evidence in your father memories. If you are a man who struggles with masculinity and what it means to be a good husband and
father, you'll find clues to the source of your struggles when you
inspect your father memories. If you are having difficulty relating
to authority figures or experiencing God as a loving father, you'll
find a key to those problems in your father memories.

Even if you have no father memories, that black hole in your
past and vacuum of father-and-child experience can influence
your adult life. As counselor and author H. Norman Wright says,
"Your father is still influencing your life today—probably more
than you realize. For example, your present thoughts and feelings
about yourself and your present relationships with other men reflect your father's impact on you. So often, what a father gives to
his daughter affects her expectations toward men in her life. Similarly, what a father withholds from his daughter can also affect her
expectations toward other men."[1]

The saying "Like father like son" is a truism. The son may
pattern himself after his father's example, or he may rebel against
whatever his dad stood for, deliberately striving to be different
from him. Either way, the son is living under his father's influence,
as his father memories will plainly indicate.

Your father stamped his seal on your life, both genetically
and psychologically. Father memories can't be shaken off, grown
out of, or painted over. They can, however, be explored, comprehended, and incorporated internally in ways that lead to lasting
change. This book is dedicated to helping you make the most of
your memories.

Before exploring how father memories work, we need to talk
a little more about how dads influence their homes and their little
ones.

FATHER SETS THE STAGE

Karen's father set the stage upon which she played out the
early years of her life. He surrounded her with criticism, put-
downs, ridicule, and insecurity, and soon she took the role of "the

little girl who wasn't good enough." As time passed, that role became her entire identity.

Now she continues to play that part—but it doesn't have to be that way. The role she took as a child was one she assigned herself. It wasn't automatically given to her. That's true for us as well. Each of us decided at an early stage how to interpret our environment. Then we assigned ourselves roles that seemed to match: The Victim. Daddy's Favorite. The Peacemaker. As children we may not have had much choice about our place in the family and in the world, but because the roles we chose were ones we assigned ourselves that means that as adults we can choose healthier roles and self-identities. We can, in other words, be the people God intended. We can, like Karen, rewrite the old script and assume a positive role.

In a later chapter I will talk specifically about different kinds of fathers and how to analyze your father memories. At this point, I would like you to consider several of the most obvious family atmospheres. The list below is not exhaustive, and specific family atmospheres can overlap, so you may not find a description below that perfectly describes your experience. But as you think about family atmospheres, consider how your father contributed to the home environment in which you grew up. Make a check opposite the description of the type of home that most closely matches the unique climate of personalities and predominant values you recall as a child.

_____ *The look-good place:* Good deed, good girl; bad deed, bad boy. You were accepted or rejected on the basis of your behavior and not for who you were as a person. Today you struggle with trying to measure up—and never feel that you quite make it.

_____ *The shape-up place:* Your father (or mother, or both) was very rigid and stressed immediate obedience. Little if any time was spent communicating feelings, opinions, or the reasons behind the rules. As a result, you either became compliant and conforming or angry and rebellious. As an adult you may find it difficult to make your own decisions and communicate them.

_____ *The yo-yo factory:* You never knew what to expect next, and you were never quite sure of what your family expected from you. As an adult you will have trouble setting boundaries for yourself and will tend to alternate between tight limits and unrestrained indulgence.

_____ *The funeral home:* Pessimism ruled. You probably never learned how to play—life was to be lived properly, not enjoyed. Laughing was out of place—even smiling was suspect. As an adult you feel guilty when you feel good or when you don't take things seriously.

_____ *The toy store:* Things and pleasure were more important than people. Children brought up in this environment often are materially blessed but relationally deprived. They find mature friendships difficult to maintain, and money becomes the main factor in too many of their decisions.

_____ *High jump haven:* No matter how high you jumped, the standards were higher. Even when you did what you were told, you didn't do it quickly enough, neatly enough, cheerfully enough, or well enough to be perfectly acceptable. "Try harder, you can do better" was the family motto. As an adult you tend to procrastinate or push yourself beyond healthy limits. Perfectionism is a problem.

_____ *The pity place:* Poor you—boo hoo! No one has ever had it so bad. You can suffer for almost anything. Focusing on your problems won you the attention you craved and provided handy excuses for possible failure. As an adult you still play the role of the victim and tend to feel sorry for yourself rather than change.

_____ *The life boat:* Somebody was always there to protect you from reality. Children who grow up in an overprotective atmosphere often find it difficult as adults to take responsibility for their own actions and live in the real world.

_____ *The respectful home:* Hurray! You learned to communicate, resolve conflicts, respect others and their property, and put people before things. You were raised in an atmosphere of genuine concern, love, and consistent discipline. As an adult those things are still important to you.

Notice that only the last home offers a healthy environment for nurturing children. People who were raised by fathers who established that type of home are fortunate. What does a good father do right? In my opinion, he excels in five areas. If your father's parenting was lacking in any of the following areas, you've had to compensate as an adult.

Ask yourself the questions below regarding your father's conduct. Do so for the purpose of identifying things to be thankful for and to build on, not as a fault-finding exercise.

FIVE FOUNDATIONS OF HEALTHY FATHERING

1. *Did your father provide emotional security?* Emotional security is a foundational element in healthy child development. A child raised without emotional and physical security comes to believe that life is like walking on quicksand. People can't be trusted and risk-taking is unpredictable and dangerous. One client of mine recalls clinging to a flag pole on the first day of kindergarten because he feared going into the school. That was a typical response to life for someone who missed out on feeling secure in his early years.

2. *Did your father value you as a person?* We all entered life with one thought: "Meet my needs!" People who were not valued as children grow up deprived of the dignity and affection they deserve. Often they respond to this deficiency in one or two ways. Some adults still squawk, kick their feet, and throw tantrums to get their way and elicit

the attention they crave, even though it is negative attention. Others battle a deep sense of inadequacy and pull inward, feeling unaccepted and unworthy, and find it a struggle to develop intimacy in their relationships. Their thinking goes like this: "Since I'm not that valuable anyway, why should anybody listen or care or treat me as special?" A young woman who came to me for counseling had let herself be dragged through the gutter of life, never understanding that she was valuable and lovable *even though* her father sent the opposite message. To deepen the tragedy, she had little ability to comprehend that a God in heaven could really care for and value her.

3. *Did your father teach you healthy touching?* The skin is the largest sense organ in the body. Touch brings pleasure or pain. My wife, Donna, knows that when she rubs my back or massages my feet I purr like a kitten. Touch connects people in a way nothing else does. It is an expression of sensual love, tender affection, and brotherly concern. If your father abused the gift of touch, or did not offer touch, you have been set up for problems—women especially. Ross Campbell says in his book *How to Really Love Your Child*, "In all my reading and experience, I have never known one sexually disoriented person who had a warm, loving, and affectionate father."[2]

4. *Did your father set boundaries and enforce them with consistent discipline?* My friends and I once attempted to play volleyball without clear boundary lines for the court—a frustrating experience. After the first volley both sides were arguing about whether the ball landed in or out. It's a great way to develop childish behavior at an adult party! The point is, clearly established boundary lines give us the freedom to function without confusion and tension. Behavioral and relational boundaries give freedom and limits, protection and safety.

   Children routinely test the boundaries and argue about the limits, but they want and need them. When those guidelines are enforced by firm, loving, and consistent discipline the child can more easily bridge the gap from childishness to self-discipline and self-control. Loving discipline leading to self-discipline is a key to healthy self-esteem. Individuals who do not establish and enforce healthy interpersonal boundaries set themselves up for others to take advantage of them. They develop all sorts of relational problems as adults.

5. *Did your father teach you the right values and help you build a belief system that leads to wise, balanced, and moral living?* Was right from wrong explained and modeled by your father? Distorted values lead to neuroticism, despair, and failure. In his book on building self-esteem in children, James Dobson lists values that lead to emotional and physical health: "The Bible provides the key to God's value system for mankind, and in my judgment, it is composed of six all-important principles. They are: (1) devotion to God; (2) love for mankind; (3) respect for authority; (4) obedience to divine commandments; (5) self-discipline and self-control and (6) humbleness of spirit. These six concepts are from the hand of the Creator, Himself, and are absolutely valid and relevant for our lives."[3]

Not surprisingly, Dobson credits his own father for the values that were instilled in him as a child and wrote this tribute on the dedication page: "This book is dedicated in deepest respect to my father, whose influence on my life has been profound. I watched him closely throughout my childhood, yet he never disappointed me. Not once did I see him compromise his inner convictions and personal ethics. Thus, his values became my values and his life charted the path for my own. Now it is my task, in turn, to be found worthy of the two little ones who call me 'Dad.'"[4]

That is the way it is supposed to work. Hurray for fathering at its best!

FATHER MEMORIES REVISITED

Karen's father failed to impart the values mentioned above. So when she came in for counseling and examined her father memories, that was a turning point in her life. For the first time she had a clear picture of how her father had inadvertently set her up for failure in relationships with men, and she learned how to break free from that destructive pattern.

When Karen first came to me for help she did not have the foggiest concept of what security and love from a man really meant. She had a trail of broken relationships, rejections, and disappointments with men that made even talking to a male counselor an act of courage.

Like a bumper car at the fair, she bounced from one man's arms to another, looking for "love" and coming away empty. And it wasn't that those men didn't really care for Karen—it was that she didn't understand the ingredients necessary for a healthy relationship with a man.

Here are some phrases pulled from her early father memories. Notice that Karen used an impersonal pronoun in place of "Dad," or even "my father," to avoid identifying in any way with the man whom she despised. Yet she desperately wanted to love and be loved by him.

> "I didn't think he really wanted me around."
> "I tried everything to get his attention."
> "In his home"—notice she didn't say "our home"—"little girls were to be seen and not heard. And boys were more valuable than girls."

Karen's father had carved destructive messages into the life of his daughter. Her private logic told her, "No matter how hard you try, you will never feel wanted, secure, and safe." Years later, the message was still lit up like a neon sign. Karen ended up spending years searching for security by running from pillar to post, or more literally from Bob to Sam to what's-his-name, trying to fill that father-void. The more numerous the relationships that crumbled, the more insecure she felt.

Some fathers offered security, warmth, and limits, and we called them "Daddy." Others pulled away and were emotionally distant, and we called them "Father." Others were hard and harsh, and we called them "the old man." And some were simply gone, and we were never sure what to call them.

FATHER MEMORIES—A LESSON IN EMOTIONAL GENETICS

Father memories are like emotional genes. They provide a thread that weaves together your view of yourself, your relationships, and God. Yet unlike biological genetics, you are not trapped by the imprinting of your father memories or past conditioning.

Your *perception* of your father memories is the most important thing you need to consider. In fact, close investigation reveals that we tend to add to, subtract from, or simply fabricate memories to fit the way we view life. Here's the process.

I'm early in the forty-something decade of life. I was fortunate to have wonderful parents who encouraged me throughout my life, but when I look into my memory bank I pull up those father memories that are consistent with my own perception of how I experience reality today. For instance, I recall that my dad has always had a preoccupation with bike safety, and, later in my life, about making sure that I had enough gas in the car. When I was a child I'm sure he was happiest when I was riding my bike around in small, safe, concentric circles in the confines of the backyard. But let's face it—going in circles can get old fast when you're six and ready to leave everyone in the dust.

In particular, I remember the day I announced that I wanted to ride my bike in the street. You would have thought I was going overseas to travel Europe alone!

This specific father memory is revealing of the Randy Carlson who travels the country today. I remember my dad's telling me about the terrible things that could happen to little boys who rode their bikes in the streets. I recall some suggestions about the possibility of being run over, being hit by a car pulling out of a driveway, or perhaps falling off and getting badly hurt—all good admonitions for a six year old to remember. But why do I still remember that discussion thirty-five years later? Because it is consistent with the way I view life today.

My careful, cautious personality is revealed in that memory. The temperament I was born with and the environment in which I grew up worked together to reinforce my guarded approach to life. I still catch myself looking over my shoulder or mentally rehearsing a list of cautions before I venture into a new experience. I almost always keep my gas tank above the half-full mark. And I seriously doubt that my own kids will ever have an accident about which they can legitimately ask, "Why didn't you warn me?"

The consistency between my father memories and the man I am today is more than coincidence. But I am not trapped by my cautious temperament. I have learned to control and overrule those tendencies when I need to in order to assume healthy risks and move on in life. I have learned to make my memories work for me. So can you.

THE LITTLE BOY OR GIRL YOU ONCE WERE, YOU STILL ARE

In your father memories you will see an unerring reflection of the person you are today. That new awareness and understanding of your personality and philosophy of life can lead you to lasting change. As I guide you on an exploration of your own father memories, we will also look together at the recollections of some of my clients, personal friends, relatives, and seminar attendees.* And we will take a look at the lifestyles and behaviors of the rich or famous and check out "the rest of the story" behind their success—the memories that reveal much about who they are today.

When I was a young man, I had the opportunity of meeting Corrie ten Boom, the noted speaker and author whose faith survived life in a concentration camp during the Holocaust. Corrie was dedicated to serving others. She and other members of her family risked or gave their lives to help Jews escape the horrors of World War II. The impact Corrie had on others, including me, was profound.

Corrie ten Boom had one smart papa. As you read her father memory, contrast her recollections with Karen's experience. The lives of both women turned out to be reflections of their father memories, for better or worse. Corrie ten Boom recalls:

> My security was assured in many ways as a child. Every night I would go to the door of my room in my nightie and call out, "Papa, I'm ready for bed." He would come to my room and pray with me before I went to sleep. I can always remember that he took time with us and would tuck the blankets around my shoulders very

---

* Names and other identifying details have been changed to protect privacy except in cases where real identities are clearly noted.

carefully, with his own characteristic precision. Then he would put his hand gently on my face and say, "Sleep well, Corrie . . . I love you."[5]

That father memory oozes with security and love. It is full of warmth and gentle touch. Boundaries are set, and Corrie's value as a person is assured. She recalls in vivid detail the way her father's love was demonstrated.

And that's the way Corrie saw her heavenly Father. The words she used and the feelings she attached to her childhood memories reveal much about the kind of woman she became. When Corrie and her sister Betsie were being held in a concentration camp, she reached back into those father memories for strength. In the most horrid conditions one can imagine, Corrie recalls:

> I sometimes remembered the feeling of my father's hand on my face. When I was lying beside Betsie on a wretched, dirty mattress in the dehumanizing prison, I would say, "O Lord, let me feel Your hand upon me . . . may I creep under the shadow of Your wings."[6]

Corrie's father was a model of love, security, and affection. Karen's father was a source of criticism and pain. In an imperfect world, some fathers leave a legacy of love and others leave a trail of heartache. But in either case, this book will help you to face your father memories for what they are and learn from them.

Exploring your father memories will be a starting point for gathering significant self-awareness and making permanent changes in your life. Like thousands of individuals who have been helped by exploring their early memories, you will discover a great deal.

- There is more in a memory than meets the eye. Your father memories reflect who you are today. Hidden in those snapshots is a picture of your present life.
- The emotions you associate with your early father memories are an unerring reflection of your emotional core.
- You don't need to be stuck in the past. The father memories that hold you back can also move you forward.

- God is not the author of confusion. He cares about your father memories—or lack of them. God can guide you to wholeness and emotional health.
- Healthy change is possible—starting today.

Let's begin by helping you get a handle on your own childhood recollections. In the next chapter I will define what is meant by a father memory and will explain how to write down and glean insights from your own memories.

NOTES

1. H. Norman Wright, *Always Daddy's Girl: Understanding Your Father's Impact on Who You Are*, ed. Ed Stewart (Ventura, Calif.: Regal, 1989), p. 10.
2. Ross Campbell, *How to Really Love Your Child* (Wheaton, Ill.: Victor, 1977), p. 73.
3. James Dobson, *Hide or Seek: How to Build Self-esteem in Your Child* (Revell, Old Tappan, N.J., 1979), p. 171.
4. Ibid., p. 5.
5. Corrie ten Boom, *In My Father's House* (Revell, Old Tappan, N. J., 1976) p. 58.
6. Ibid., p. 58.

2

WHAT DO YOU RECALL?

It will be your turn to write down a few childhood recollections at the end of this chapter, but first I want to offer some pointers that will make the process easier and more profitable. Those tips will give you a better understanding of what father memories are and the basics of interpreting what they mean. To begin, let me take you "up close and personal" and present my own earliest father memory:

> I must be about three years old. I recall sitting on my mother's lap as my dad drove us down the street toward our house. I remember looking over at my dad driving the car, and feeling secure, safe, and happy.

In retrospect, I can see that sitting on my mother's lap while the car was moving wasn't exactly a memory oozing with security. But it was 1954 and seat belts weren't yet standard safety equipment, so we'll let my parents off the hook. The key is that I *felt* secure, which brings up *tip number one:*

> Father memories are full of the emotions you had as a little child—you shouldn't worry yet about editing them through adult eyes. Simply write down what happened and how you felt —not how you think things should have been or how you think you should have felt.

27

Threads of desiring security, pleasing others, and "whatever you do, don't rock the boat" are woven through my father memories. For example, I remember

- at age eight, taking my father's special antique saxophone to school, where it was damaged by other students, then coming home from school and being worried about what my dad would think
- falling off my two-wheel bike in front of some friends and family members and feeling embarrassed
- hurting my foot but not wanting to tell my dad—I didn't want to upset him

Notice that I mention two things in each recollection: what happened and how I felt about it. That leads to *the second tip:*

> The emotion tied to the memory and your perception of the incident are as important as the event itself. Try to write down not only what happened but how you responded and felt. *The words you use to describe your memories and the feelings you attach to them say volumes about who you are and how you live today.*

In my case, the facts show that I never needed to fear my father's reaction. He was always loving and supportive. I love my dad and respect him greatly. We have a wonderful relationship. And yet when I recall father memories from my childhood, I attach the emotional thread of not feeling like I measured up and never wanting to be embarrassed.

My memories illustrate an important principle about how all father memories work: *the facts from our father memories are filtered through our personalities and perceptions of life.* Our unique fears, hopes, and interpretations of life color how we remember our childhoods. Even a present mood can affect how we describe a past event.

WHO'S RESPONSIBLE HERE?

We have been told for years by some psychological gurus to blame our parents for our emotional, relational, and spiritual warts. It's man's nature to look for a scapegoat—and parents grill up nicely on the altar of blame.

If we chop through the weeds of our past long enough, most of us can pull up a root or two that will lead back to our parents. But to make the most of your father memories, you need to recognize that memory exploration is not part of a blame game. That leads to *tip number three:*

> Use your memories for improving yourself,
> not for blaming someone else.

Children will point their fingers every which way, except toward themselves. If something breaks or spills it's everybody else's fault except the guilty party's. Even adults tend to blame others for their problems. So we shouldn't be surprised at the present wash of material that excuses the adult child at the expense of the parent. I call that syndrome the "flat tire" approach to problem solving: when things "go flat" on us we kick the tire and blame the nail in the road. But we don't need to respond that way. We can change the tire and get back on the road.

In my counseling practice I have witnessed and wept over the tragic results in adults who were raised in an unhealthy environment. They have played their memories over and over in their minds like a bad movie. I don't mean to minimize the pain of people whose parents emotionally or physically abused them. Yet I agree fully with popular author and lecturer Lee Ezell, who, after reporting her memories of life as the child of a violent alcoholic, reports as well her insightful response to the pain of the past:

> My earliest childhood memories are of the family running for cover as my crazed father climbed the steps from his basement dwelling. After physical abuse, screams, and cries, one of us would make it to the phone and call the police for help. Language was vile, and tempers ran hot in our household. This was the climate I grew up in deep in Philadelphia's inner city. . . .
>
> To use the terms of pop psychology, I would say that I am a codependent ACOA (Adult Children of Alcoholics) in recovery from

a dysfunctional family whose inner child was apparently adopted out. While these terms might explain my behavior, they don't excuse my behavior. I can't blame my mother for my cellulite because she was the one who taught me to swallow my feelings and chase them down with a milk shake. And, yes, my dad was a poor model of a father, but I do not have to be crippled in my relationship to God the Father all of my adult life because of my earthly father.

I believe my parents were responsible for what they did then; I am responsible for what I do now.[1]

I spent time with Lee at a convention and witnessed firsthand how a person can overcome a painful past and have a tremendous impact for good on the world. The bottom line is what we decide to do with the memories we have, not how eagerly or accurately we cast the blame. As I've said before, in dealing with father memories the goal is growth, not rummaging around in the past in order to pull out excuses for our present behavior.

Your Earliest Memory, Please

How you record your memories, what about them is significant, and what you rightly need to do with your memories are all important, but so, too, is the time frame of those memories. That leads to *tip number four:*

> As you prepare to write down some father memories of your own, try to recall your earliest and most vivid memories. If possible, try to go back before the age of eight.

Anything will work. A father memory doesn't have to be a major event or traumatic experience. Be sure, however, that you are considering your own memory and not just a story you've been told by others. (If you can remember feeling a specific emotion or can see a specific picture of the scene in your mind it is probably a true memory.)

Just how far back can a person remember with accuracy? That question comes up often. Some of us have trouble remembering what we had for lunch, let alone a far away and long ago father memory. In general, the earlier your father memory the better, within reason, but you do not have to think back *this* far . . .

The Ultimate Early Memory

While I was doing a radio talk show in Chicago I hit upon the wildest memory I've ever heard and the earliest on record to date. A lady with an animated voice claimed she could remember *being born!* Telling me the memory in private would be one thing. It was another to describe the sights and sounds in messy detail before about a half-million people listening by radio. The astonished look on the studio engineer's face told the story, and I felt the listeners must have agreed, that I had a nut-case on the air. But I wasn't so sure.

This lady "recalled" the experience of being born in living color. She remembered seeing a swirling stream of lights and then the feel of being forced through a dark tunnel that finally led to the arms of the waiting doctor. By this time the program listeners were either hooked big time or had switched the dial.

The Truth and Nothing but the Truth?

Did she actually remember being born? Not likely. But that is only half the point. To some degree your memories will tell something about you, whether or not they tell something about true history. In this respect, it really doesn't matter if your father memories are pure fact or partly fiction.

The important thing is what a person *says* he remembers and how he *feels* about it. So I told this lady that of the thousands of memories I had heard, hers was the earliest memory on record, if not the most unique. While I tried to still the rumble of laughter coming from the engineering booth, I asked, "Do you see yourself as being creative, sensitive, and concerned with detail?"

"Yes, that's me," she responded. "How did you know?"

How did I know? Check the detail in her memory and her sensitivity to sight and sound. This is a woman who has emotional feelers that could pick up an experience at forty yards. She could hear an ant cough at a picnic. A person who remembers being born wouldn't quickly forget being offended or complimented by her fourth grade teacher. As for the creativity—let's say that was just a hunch.

When you write down your memories try to be as specific and accurate as possible. Always seek the truth, but don't be discouraged if your parents or siblings don't remember that it happened exactly that way.

Father memories are your personal picture of the world as you know it. And we all have our own way of drawing a picture—each is personal, private, and distorted.

We often manufacture in our minds those things and perceptions that help us make sense of our world. If that requires distorting, adding, deleting, or ignoring the truth, the mind bends the rules with great ease. The Bible confirms that we are not always honest with ourselves. Jeremiah 17:9 lays it out bluntly: "The heart is deceitful above all things and beyond cure. Who can understand it?"

I am convinced that a lie repeated often enough takes on its own distorted truth. Perhaps that is why Scripture speaks about the importance of controlling our thinking. As you consider your father memories try to recall the simple truth about the way things were—not the way you wish they could have been or the way you may have recast your memories to rationalize your response to the past.

Try It On for Size

Take a moment now to write your own father memory—either in the space below or on a separate sheet of paper. Here is summary of the pointers I have mentioned:

1. The earlier the memory, the better.
2. The more father memories, the better.
3. Tell what happened—specific, vivid events, not generalities.
4. Tell how you felt about what happened.

It might also be helpful to follow this general format as you write:

I REMEMBER _____

_____

_____

THE CLEAREST PART OF MY MEMORY IS _____

_____

_____

AS I THINK ABOUT THE MEMORY I FEEL _____

_____

_____

If you can't think of a father memory, don't get discouraged. That's more common than you might think. About 15 percent of those who attend an early memory seminar can't write down an early memory without further help. Hang in there—before you go too far a memory or two will likely pop up. When it does, stop reading and get it down in print.

WHAT YOU REMEMBER IS WHO YOU ARE

Kevin Leman and I began the book *Unlocking the Secrets of Your Childhood Memories* with this promise: "Tell us about your earliest childhood memories and we'll tell you about yourself today.

"We can confidently make this declaration because WHO YOU ARE TODAY . . . YOUR BASIC PERSONALITY . . . THE SECRET TO YOUR ENTIRE OUTLOOK ON LIFE . . . IS HIDDEN WITHIN YOUR EARLIEST CHILDHOOD MEMORIES."[2]

I made those statements, and stand by them, because each person has a selective memory—he subconsciously sorts through his memories with creative consistency and recalls or recasts those that fit his present outlook. We balance our past and present by remembering only those events from early childhood that are consistent with our present view of ourselves and the world around us.

In *Family Matters* Daniel Gottlieb talks about understanding our memories in the context of a painting. He writes, "Broad strokes are placed on those portraits-of-the-world by our early experiences, both with our parents and with our loved ones. Peers and other significant people add further brush strokes. For most of us, the paint dries early."[3]

Although your basic picture of the world took shape years ago, personal growth has resulted in some changes in your interpretation of the scene. Therefore you can look at the past with a more mature appraisal now than as a child. And your picture of the past will be filtered though the eyes of the person you are now.

So in your father memories you will see an unerring reflection of the person you are today. And that new awareness and understanding of your personality and philosophy of life can lead you to lasting change. Where should you look to find the meaning in your father memories? Considering the following possibilities will help you get started.

PUTTING FATHER IN HIS PLACE

To understand the meaning of your memories look for the obvious, basic clues first. The way we men related to our fathers as little boys will give us a snapshot of how we view manhood. Similarly, women will find in the way they related to their fathers as children patterns of how they relate to men as adults, especially in marriage. Consider the following questions:

- What place does your father take in your memories? Is he close? Absent? Distant?
- What is the chemistry between you and your dad? Affection? Fear? Encouragement?
- What role do you assume? Being in control? Pleasing him? Rebelling?

During a recent father memory seminar an attractive young woman came up to me and asked if I could explain the significance of her father's role in her early memory. As you read her memory, take a few guesses about Norma's view of life as an adult:

> I remember going out to help my dad shovel the snow that had fallen on our sidewalk following a giant snowstorm. The shovels were out in the garage so we had to make the long trek through the deep snow. I followed my dad—stretching my legs as far as I could in order to land in each of his footsteps. I knew I could make it, and I did. It felt great to see that I could do it.

If you guessed that Norma is a woman with a mission you are correct. Her memory reveals it, and her lifestyle proves it. She works sixty hours a week to climb the corporate ladder while trying to hold down a romantic relationship—an arrangement many women are discovering is costly. Norma hopes to get married someday, but admits she's not sure how to do it all on her current schedule. Norma's father is her role model for success; she does not identify with her mother sitting in a cozy house. The memory snapshot of Norma following in her father's footsteps is not just coincidence.

Each of the following guiding thoughts is present in Norma's father memory:

1. Hard work is good.
2. Working together is good.
3. If you want to succeed in life plan on stretching some.
4. Quitters never win.
5. Men can be trusted and are able leaders.

LIKE FATHER, LIKE SON?

Like Norma, Thomas Watson, Jr., had some big steps to follow. Young Watson was the Jr. to Thomas Watson, Sr., the founder of the billion-dollar IBM empire. And the junior Watson "got it into his head" that he had to follow in his father's footsteps to the end. He spent a lifetime jumping hurdles and pushing himself in order to measure up to what his father memories were telling him about living a successful life. In his book *Father, Son, & Co.* Thomas Watson, Jr., writes about his childhood:

> I never remember, when I was growing up, Father coming right out and saying, "I'd really like to have you follow me in this business." In fact, looking at me then, he probably found it hard to imagine a less likely successor. But I got it into my head that the old man wanted me to come into IBM, take it over, and run the whole deal. The very idea made me miserable. One day after school, when I was about twelve, I sat on a curb thinking about my father. What precipitated it I don't know, but by the time I got home I was in tears. My mother asked me what was wrong and I said, "I can't do it. I can't go to work at IBM."[4]

Watson's father memory reveals a man with an intense emotional struggle. It gives us a glimpse into a classic father-son dilemma. Should he go after what he wants in life, or should he follow this thing in his head that says his father expects him to join the company? Watson did grow up to become a successful CEO for IBM, but his memory suggests that he never really enjoyed the pressure of being at the top. Notice the repetition of the thought "I can't do it" and "The very idea made me miserable."

At the age of fifty-six, while still in the prime of his business life, Thomas Watson, Jr., confirms the little boy's reluctance:

> Enough was going wrong by 1970 that I started to daydream about a very different kind of life. In the top drawer of my desk, mixed with memos about key business issues and old letters from Dad, I had a secret list that I'd take out and look at when nobody was around. On it were adventures I wanted to have: climbing the Matterhorn was first, then learning to fly a helicopter, going on safari, sailing to the Arctic and around Cape Horn, and making a single-handed voyage—to anywhere. I also wanted time to enjoy myself with my wife and my children. My zest for business was evaporating fast. We'd built IBM into a seven-billion-dollar-a-year giant, and in my heart of hearts I felt that I'd taken it as far as I wanted to go.[5]

THE PARTS PEOPLE PLAY

Many of us, like Thomas Watson, will spend a lifetime trying to play out the role decided upon long ago. As you review your own father memories, look for the thread that pulls them together. It will be a theme that makes sense to you and fits your underlying identity.

Life roles can be uncovered through memory exploration. The part you play, sometimes referred to as your life theme or life-style, represents how you see yourself fitting into the world around you. Think about the father memory you just wrote down, and ask yourself, "What does it say about my role in life?" "If I were to be type-cast in a similar role today, what would that role be?" Here are several typical roles that may be found in your father memories:[6]

Pleasers   — need the approval of others
Controllers — want it "my way or no way"
Drivers   — say "Get out of my way, there are things to do"

Getters	— focus on me, me, me, using others to satisfy self
Babies	— manipulate others through their charm
Martyrs	— are silent or not-so-silent sufferers
Victims	— are willing to suffer for anything

The repetitious appearance of a person, an emotion, a location, or even a smell may lead you to personal insights. Each father memory will accurately tell you something about yourself, but not everything about yourself. Looking for consistent patterns through an assortment of father memories will fill in the missing pieces. For example, were you an observer or a participator? Were you a giver or a taker? Did you feel adventurous or fearful? Not all of the questions I have mentioned apply to every father memory, but any one of them could expose telltale patterns or habits.

If you uncover a negative theme, don't despair. For example, under some circumstances you may truly act like a baby in order to get your way, but that is not the whole story. The pop psychology idea that there is one "true you" is a myth.

For instance, you may have thrown tantrums like a baby to control your parents, yet take a different approach entirely to communicate with your spouse. Or you may assume the role of the insignificant pleaser at home, yet take an assertive, confident stance in your role at work. We all relate differently to our bosses than to our subordinates, to our parents than to our children, to our friends than to strangers. In short, we are capable of assuming many roles, even simultaneously. And we can transfer a positive pattern of response from one role to another, from one relationship to another. You are not permanently locked into one role—skills you already possess can liberate you. Thus there is always potential for change and personal growth.

Don't be concerned if you don't figure everything out quickly. The principles of memory exploration are simple, but not simplistic. In the next chapter we'll talk more about the law of creative consistency as it relates to understanding your father memories.

NOTES

1. Lee Ezell, in *What My Parents Did Right,* by Gloria Gaither (Nashville: Star-Song, 1991), p. 218.
2. Randy Carlson and Kevin Leman, *Unlocking the Secrets of Your Childhood Memories* (Nashville: Thomas Nelson, 1989), p. 11.
3. Daniel Gottieb, *Family Matters* (New York: E. P. Dutton, 1991), p. 9.
4. Thomas Watson, Jr., *Father, Son & Co.* (New York: Bantam, 1990), p. 26.
5. Ibid., p. 390.
6. Adapted in part from H. H. Mosak, "Lifestyle," in *Techniques for Behavior Change,* ed. A. G. Nikelly (Springfield, Ill.: Charles C. Thomas, 1971), p. 77.

3

THE SEARCH FOR MEANING IN YOUR MEMORIES

Jerilyn, a slim brunette in a bright cotton dress, greeted me cheerfully as she drew me aside following a seminar. It was obvious she had some questions about this father memory business. "I wrote down the first three memories that came to mind, like you said. But I have some questions," she began. "Maybe you should go back over what you called the law of creative consistency."

"Simply put, the law of creative consistency is: People remember only those events from early childhood that are consistent with their present view of themselves and their world around them," I explained. "That's the way we keep our past and our present in balance and avoid what the stuffed-shirts call *cognitive dissonance*—mental imbalance from conflicting inner data that would drive us crazy. In other words, the three father memories you jotted down will reveal the person you are today. Because your basic personality, your underlying identity, is a permanent and unalterable part of you the memories you jotted down will consistently mirror who you are."

BUT WHAT ABOUT THE INCONSISTENCIES?

Jeri raised one eyebrow, then remarked frankly, "Either I don't get it, or I don't buy it!"

"Even if there are seemingly many contradictions, the memories will be held together by a common thread. It really works, Jeri," I said with enthusiasm as I felt a lecture coming on. Fortunately for her, I got hold of myself before stepping up to my imaginary microphone and opted to shut up and listen. "What specifically appears to be the problem?" I asked. "Let's take a look at those memories together."

Jeri's personality must be akin to the Bereans in the book of Acts, who searched through the Bible and thought through the things they heard before they would accept their value. She wasn't about to accept all this about father memories without clarification. And that was soon to follow.

Here are the father memories she found confusing at first:

1. I remember feeling very excited as I was going fishing with my dad when I was around four or five. He told me to put on a life jacket, and I didn't really want to—but I did it anyway so that we could get on with the fun. I figured if Dad said to do it, it must be something I needed to do.
2. When I was really little I used to climb up on my dad's lap and "help" him play the accordion. I remember being happy and giggling when he bounced his knee to the music. I feel lucky to have had so many good times with my dad; we had a lot of fun together.
3. One time when we bought a new car Dad took all of us kids out for a test drive. When we reached the edge of town on the blacktop road Dad began to floor the gas pedal. I was in the back seat with my brother, looking over Dad's shoulder at the speedometer as it topped 100!

Jeri went on to share more details that came to mind about the three incidents from her childhood, then teased, "If what you say is true, I must be schizophrenic—or my father was!"

"Tell me what you see in these stories," I grinned and replied.

"In the first memory I'm a little rebellious but give in, while in the second two I'm passively going along for the ride. Sometimes we're outdoors, sometimes inside. Sometimes my brother and sister were there, too, and in other memories Dad and I are alone," Jeri noted. "And if you take the first one out of context, my Dad is careful enough for safety precautions—but then he's daring enough for a drag race. Where's the consistency? I come up with $1 + 1 = 3$, which makes perfect nonsense!"

On the surface Jeri's memories did seem to contradict one another, and she was understandably confused. In the same way, your recollections may not appear to fit together at first. But they will fit together if you remember that properly interpreting your father memories hinges on the principle that *you are the most important person in your father memories—not your father.*

Your memories tell your story through your eyes, reflecting your character, not his. In other words, as you inspect your father memories turn your eyes upon yourself as the center of attention and ask, "What do these father memories reveal about me and my style of relating to others and my world?"

You may think, as Jeri did, that your memories just don't add up. Maybe in one instance your dad is angry, in the next he's quiet, and in the third he's not even present. But don't let changing roles and people confuse you. The details surrounding the events and the actions of others only set the stage for the main character—you.

If you can't find the thread that connects your patchwork of recollections, it may help you to ask yourself two questions concerning your memories: First, what's the clearest part of the memory? And second, how did you feel at that point?

I like to think of father memories as personal home movies that we wrote, produced, and filmed ourselves. It helps to freeze the movie on the clearest frame. By articulating the emotion associated with that one clearest part of the memory, you will have a better grasp of the significance of the whole.

When I asked Jeri how she felt when her father pretended to be A. J. Foydt at Indy and raced down the road, she replied, "Oh, I thought it was great fun."

Bingo. The consistency lay in Jeri's *emotional perception* of the events, not in the events themselves. Jeri's response fit perfectly with her personality. The mental snapshots she had taken depicted her as a fun-loving child who liked to do things and enjoyed being involved in activities with her father. Notice that all of her memories involved doing something and that she repeated the idea of having fun: "to get on with the fun," "we had a lot of fun," and "it was great fun."

In the same way, you, too, need to look for recurring phrases, persons, or feelings in the memories you wrote out. Remember that your emotions are often the key to unlocking the memory. When I pointed out the recurring phrases in Jeri's father memories she immediately agreed that they fit in with who she is today. She is still happiest when she is doing something with one or two people she cares about. She enjoys the excitement of new experiences. Jeri's memories indicated that she had a healthy, loving relationship with her father—and that the same shared companionship exists in her marriage today.

After I described the patterns in her father memories I could see that Jeri was busy thinking. "Let me see if I have this right now by saying it a different way," she said. "My grandmother was an artist, and when I was little I used to watch as she did her oil paintings. She would show me how the trees had just a little of the sky color, and the water had a hint of ground colors, and so on. Even though the trees or clouds or fences were entirely different objects they were all painted from the same palette of unique colors that Grandma mixed up. My father memories remind me of that—even though they are different pieces of the painting they are all colored by the same perceptions and values. My unique personality palette remains consistent. Is that right?"

Exactly. Jeri's word picture is a beautiful analogy of the way the law of creative consistency works. You may find, as she did, that sharing your memories with someone else will help you interpret your memories. A friend may be able to see a pattern or notice a key thought as you talk things through. Therefore I strongly encourage you to talk to a trusted friend about your father memories if you are still unsure about what they might mean.

WHERE TO START LOOKING

The following exercise will help you get started on your own memory safari. In addition to the themes or characteristics I've already mentioned, hunt down the answers to the following questions. Ask yourself:

1. *Was I active or passive?* Active memories tend to come from active people; passive memories from passive people.

2. *Was I an observer or a participant?* You take the same approach to life today.

3. *What was my physical posture?* Your physical posture is a subtle but significant element in the father memory. If you were looking away, not holding eye contact, slouching, or fidgeting, that would indicate low self-esteem or insecurity. If big people are looking down at you in your memories, then authority figures are still important to you today. If you cross your arms in front of you, walling out others, then you still shut certain people out today. Your posture generally reflects your true inner attitude.

4. *Was I alone or with others when I was happiest as a child?* Loners have "I" memories of activities they did alone, whereas people-persons remember "we" kinds of activities from their childhoods.

5. *Was I concerned with people, things, activities, or ideas?* What concerned you most as a child will likely be what holds your interest today.

6. *Were you confrontational or a peacemaker?* Those behaviors will tell you something about which style of relating you gravitate toward as an adult.

7. *Was there detail, color, or sound?* If any of those elements appear in your father memories, congratulations. They tend to come from creative people.

THE MEMORIES SAY SOMETHING—SO WHAT!

Jeri's memories revealed that she thought for herself and reached her own conclusions, as when she quickly concluded it was best to put on the life jacket. Her memories also indicated a tendency toward rebellion; she initially resisted the life jacket and felt no qualms about breaking the speed limit. Therefore, it was no surprise to me that she was comfortable in challenging my authority and thinking through my instructions before accepting their value. And because her relationship with her father had been open and honest, it was no surprise either that she was asking me direct questions. Like the little girl who wanted to get on to the fishing, or who enjoyed bouncing on her daddy's leg, or who had fun speeding down the road, the adult Jeri was someone who liked to keep things moving. So I could have anticipated her next remarks.

"OK, Randy, I'm willing to agree that the insights from my memories obey the law of creative consistency, yet I'm still puzzled about their value. What you said about my personality is true, but it's nothing new. I could have told you before I even wrote down the memories that I like to be active. All of my friends and family already know that I enjoy new projects and a little adventure in life. That's just the way I am. And I'm well aware that I can be selectively rebellious. So what?"

Jeri paused, realizing how funny her last phrase had sounded, and we both burst out laughing. "I didn't mean 'I'm rebellious—so what?' in a defiant way," she quickly explained, blushing. "What I meant is, what difference does it make in my life today if I'm already aware of those tendencies and know when they generally surface?"

SELF-KNOWLEDGE IS THE FIRST STEP TOWARD SELF-IMPROVEMENT

I told Jeri that many people lack the self-awareness to accurately identify their personal strengths and weaknesses in the way that she did. People often feel some confusion over self-identify and the dynamics that work against personal growth. For them, exploring their father memories gives them insight and a tool for gaining new understanding of the patterns affecting their present lives. Self-knowledge is the first step to self-improvement.

I explained to Jeri that hidden in her father memories were keys to understanding her relationships and her style of responding to problems, conflict, intimacy, and success. Moreover, as she heard the father memories of others, she would be able to answer such questions as these:

- Why do I have trouble communicating with my husband? Ask your husband to describe his father memories, and you will have some clues.
- Why do some of my co-workers drive me crazy? Ask your co-workers to share a father memory, and their personalities will show themselves in the words they use and the particular memories they describe.
- What are my teenagers thinking about life? Ask your teenagers to report a father memory, and what they are thinking

will reveal itself. (Steve's story in chapter 9, "Putting Father Memories to Work," is a great example.)

As we have already seen, because of the law of creative consistency, father memories mirror life themes and expectations. For example, you may find that you consistently

- strive to please your father and seek his approval
- allow yourself to be dominated or intimidated by an angry or extremely competent father
- discover a warmth and acceptance in your relationship with Dad that leads to comfortable closeness with men today
- adopt an "I'm in trouble, come rescue me, Daddy" mentality of depending upon others to solve life's problems
- expect the worst and plan to get into trouble over almost every decision you make

Denial or self-deception are also common problems, but childhood memories will help to expose your true emotions, identify relational problems, and develop a road map for permanent change.

I receive hundreds of letters each month, and I read them all. I usually pay little attention, however, to those that come to me unsigned or without a return address (hate mail is usually written in yellow ink by chicken lips who are afraid to call or talk in person). One letter, which came with only a first name attached, was an exception. It took tremendous courage to write the father memory described in the letter, and I regret very much that it was impossible for me to reply to it. The letter was from a woman I'll call Cheryl. It shows how one childhood memory can expose what a person tries hard to bury or deny.

> The little girl had found a fragile baby sparrow that had fallen from its nest. *Poor thing,* she thought, *I'm sorry you've fallen and are hurt and lonely. I can help you. I know I can.* She gently picked up the weak little bird and covered it with her other hand to protect it and give it a feeling of warmth and security. I'll take it to Daddy. He'll know what to do, she decided.

But when she entered the house she knew immediately this was not the time to ask Daddy anything. She could smell alcohol in the room and wanted to run back outside, but it was too late. Her Daddy saw her and said, "What are you holding? Bring it here."

She hesitatingly showed her father the sweet invalid she had found. "Daddy can we help this little bird? It just needs some food and love."

"Why did you pick up this bird?" father said sternly, his words slurred together. "Don't you know that once you touch a fallen bird, the mother will never accept it again—it's going to die because of you."

The little girl didn't believe it. "No! I can help it, I know I can!" she shouted.

This made her father very angry, and he forced the baby bird from the small hand. With a forceful shove he pushed her down and staggered outside. The little girl's heart was broken into pieces and sadness overwhelmed her. She ran after her father, tears pouring down her swollen face.

When she got outside she saw her father standing awkwardly, staring down at the asphalt drive. There the little bird lay crushed, where he had thrown it to the ground. . . .

Not a happy story—one of the saddest ones I know. But it is a story I believe because I lived it. With shaking hand I'm writing this. The past few weeks this memory has been with me, waking me from my sleep, reminding me of the frailty of life in my daily moments as I see pain around me.

My heart is tender toward others in pain, but I can't express the paralyzing fear when I try to help. . . . I'm scared of hurting them, I'm tired of hearing of pain, and sad because I want to tell them I know what pain is. But I can't say it. I'm the cheerful encourager who lives a fairy tale life with a wonderful husband and beautiful children.

I love the Lord, and He is my dearest friend. His faithful love has given me the comfort I need when I feel like—like the little girl, but also like the fallen sparrow. I want so much for someone to protect me and love me. . . .

Oh well, I'm very thankful for all the beautiful blessings God has given. Yes, there were difficult days growing up, but that was in the past. A whole other life ago. This is now, and every day I thank God for His love and the joy of a new day.

These aren't things I can talk to anyone about because, really, that sad little girl doesn't exist anymore today.

Sincerely,
Cheryl

Cheryl, if you are reading this book, please write and include your address so that I can correspond. In the meantime, let me share several important points from Cheryl's letter that will help you think about the validity and significance of your own father memories.

Cheryl is a compassionate and creative young woman. She is still seeking the approval and acceptance of her father. In fact, while living with her "wonderful husband" she is still looking for someone "to protect and love" her. Her desire to help others is exceeded only by her fear of rejection and loss. She is frozen by fear and chooses to live in a "fairyland" rather to risk exposing her true feelings to others. The letter was a safe way to share the story, and I'm sure it helped.

But there was work yet undone. After pouring out her pain from childhood and admitting that she is still struggling with those issues, Cheryl discounted her entire letter by saying, "But that was in the past. A whole other life ago." That's just not true—for Cheryl, or for any of us. What happened in the past *matters*. Denial doesn't work. Denying the impact of your father memories will rob you of the chance to find healing and hope for today. Facing father memories will help you cut through the wall you have placed around painful problems and will give you insight into the real issues underlying your emotions, even when you can't otherwise seem to put a finger on them.

Dan, for example, was a reserved executive in his early thirties. As a successful and confident salesman he got along well with his clients, his colleagues, and his boss, the vice president of sales. That is, at first. But lately, tension had been building up between him and many of his co-workers, and he wasn't sure why. Father memories helped him sort out his feelings and solve the problems.

Dan reported that things had begun to change at work when a female salesperson, Jane, was transferred to their all-male division. After that, Dan explained, he seemed to get irritated at his boss more often, but he wasn't sure why. All he knew was that he was overreacting to situations.

A look at Dan's early childhood revealed that he had grown up in a family with two brothers and one sister. When I asked him to tell me something about his family relationships, especially the relationship between his sister and his father, Dan recalled:

My sister, Debbie, insisted on being treated just like we were—anything we could do, she could do. Except she didn't want to do any of the dirty work. She just wanted the fun part, or work that brought praise and attention. She didn't do her share, and we covered for her. For example, we lived on a ranch and worked cattle with quarter horses. Debbie loved horses and could ride as well as any of us. But when the windchill was forty below zero and it was time to do chores, well, then the horses were ours to take care of. Sometimes we complained, but it didn't do any good. Dad always took her part.

Just listening to himself tell the story out loud was enough to help Dan realize that buried resentments against his sister and unresolved frustration over the way his father did things were at the heart of his current difficulties in dealing with people at work. Although Dan had tried to keep childhood hurts locked inside, they had leaked out into present situations where they didn't belong. But as Dan acknowledged the feelings he had buried or denied for a long time, they came out in the open where they could be resolved.

Dan's eyes lit up as he remarked, "So that's it—that's why I overreacted the other day!" He went on to explain. "At the company, every sales representative is responsible for washing his company car nearly every day—it's company policy to insure that we make a good impression on the field. The other day one of the guys drove Jane's car around for her and ran it through the car wash so she wouldn't have to get out in the wind. It was a kind thing for him to do, but it made me so angry I could hardly work the rest of the day. And I was mad at myself for letting such a little thing upset me."

That incident touched a raw nerve in Dan's inner life. He reacted to it with the intensity due past wrongs, not the intensity due present reality. As Dan took a closer look at the situation at work, he realized that Jane was eager to do her share and often made helpful gestures to brighten the day of those around her. That, in turn, fostered goodwill and return acts of kindness from co-workers. And his boss was conducting business as usual, handling minor disputes with fairness, not simply taking Jane's part. So Dan rightly concluded that the problem was with him, not them.

Things improved at work right away. Eventually Dan found the courage to talk with Debbie about his childhood. To his surprise, Debbie opened up and told him that as the only girl among boys she had often felt left out of the fraternity of fun. When the boys loaded up to go hunting, she was left behind to make dinner. When their family attended every basketball and football game the boys played in, she sat in the stands. (There were no successful sports programs for girls in their school at the time.) And when the boys were encouraged to achieve anything they established as a goal in their careers, she was told that teaching was a nice profession for women—you could always find work wherever your husband decided to live.

Dan and Debbie learned a lot about each another as a result of their heart-to-heart talk. Dan had not realized that Debbie had ever been left out of anything until she related her own memories. As a result of their conversation, Dan and Debbie grew closer and became more supportive of one another.

The unfolding of his father memories was the starting point of significant change in Dan's life. Memories can work in the same way for you.

Exploring your father memories will be profitable for you whether you, like Dan, need fresh insight into relational problems, or, like Jeri, already recognize the behaviors or attitudes that have made your life unpleasant. Just as Dan identified emotions prompted by past events that were consistent with his reactions in the present, so you will find consistencies that can lead to personal growth.

In the next chapter we will talk more specifically about different types of fathers and the imprint they leave on their children. If you read a description that reflects your upbringing, keep in mind that what you recall from your childhood doesn't have to be reality for you today. Like Jeri, you can decide to learn new techniques for improving relationships. Like Dan, you can decide to change.

Part 2

Dad's Lasting Impression

4

KINDS OF FATHER MEMORIES; KINDS OF FATHERS

My father was never around for important events," Barbara said. "I remember wanting him to come to my kindergarten field day, but he couldn't make it. And Dad wasn't there when I won a 4-H award at the county fair. Come to think of it, Dad didn't even bother to show up in the delivery room when I was born—he just waited around outside and left everything to Mom! The way I see it, my father was a jerk."

THE WAY I SEE IT—OR THE WAY IT WAS?

Barbara, a hard-driving career woman carrying a brief case and about fifteen extra pounds, sought counseling because she was living out several destructive life themes. Although she did not say so directly, the statements below represented the thoughts revealed in her father memory. From her experiences with her father she had concluded:

- Men won't be there when you need them; don't trust them because they'll let you down.
- Men leave all the dirty work to women.
- Men are jerks.

But there's more to any memory than initially meets the eye. Although Barbara may have experienced legitimate disappointment in the past, the way she sees it is *not* the way it was—or is. That is because *we all have a selective memory and biased emotions that distort reality.*

You can easily prove the point for yourself. At the next family gathering ask your siblings and parents to give the details of some past family event. You will hear a different version of the same story from each person. Why? Because of the principle of selectivity.

The selective process can be a great help or a terrible burden. We choose what we remember and how we remember it. Therefore, a fearful child remembers something as simple as a lightening storm as a traumatic event, whereas an adventurous sibling may only recall what fun it was to stay up late or sleep in the basement. Many times we find what we are programmed to look for—not what is really there.

Take Barbara. In defense of Barbara's father, further conversations revealed that he had provided well for his family, had taken family vacations on a regular basis, and had never missed one of her birthday parties (although Barbara claimed that was just because her mother insisted he come). I pointed out that during the decade Barbara was born few hospitals allowed men in the delivery room, and they were surely not expected to be there. She had been projecting today's ideal of the totally involved father onto the past and was drawing conclusions about her dad that were not justified.

Barbara's remarks also betrayed her low view of traditional woman's roles, which was consistent with her pursuit of success in a predominantly male field she considered more important than marriage and motherhood. I gently suggested that Barbara's memories had given her a distorted perception of both the past and present—as is true for each of us.

Barbara's response? She became defensive and insisted, "I know what it was like to grow up in my family. *I was there!*"

Barbara carried a chip on her shoulder heavy enough to squash the life out of any friendships she might have had with men in her adult life. Many factors went into the makeup of her lifestyle. It was not simply the result of a perceived abandonment in the daddy/daughter relationship, although that strongly contributed to the lies she lived by.

To check out how this selective screening process may be tinting the family photos in your mind, ask yourself these two questions about each scene you recall:

1. *Do the details of my memory make sense in light of reality?* I had one person tell me that he remembered sliding down a hill and under his family's 1964 Ford station wagon on his sled. When I asked him to think that through, he checked it out and discovered that it would have been physically impossible for any sled carrying a child to fit under the car.

   Another woman insisted that Aunt Carol had always snubbed her, even refusing to attend her graduation. But guess whose smiling face was in the photograph of the occasion? Aunt Carol in living color. She was in the background cutting the cake at the reception following the graduation ceremony.

2. *Can other people who were in my father memory confirm, change, or add to it?* I hear many variations of the one-sided memory. You remember, for example, that Dad bought you a shiny new scooter when your brother and sisters only had old ones. But do you remember that he backed over the old one the night before while you were in bed, and felt obligated to replace it? Probably not. It seemed more special to think that he gave you the new one because you were his favorite.

   Of course, many of the times your memory plays tricks on you aren't this trivial or harmless. It pays to ask someone to fill in the rest of the story.

WHY WE DO WHAT WE DO

Barbara is following a definite plan for her life, a plan she developed early in her childhood. So are we. The things we do and say, the choices we make, and the attitudes that influence those choices are determined by the lifestyle we are following—sometimes deliberately, but often subconsciously.

The word *lifestyle* has become somewhat generalized from its original meaning. When we hear of the television show "Lifestyles of the Rich and Famous" we think of a general manner of living typical of a certain social strata. However, when I use the word *lifestyle* in this book I am not referring to riches or fame. I am speaking about how a person sees the world around him.

A friend might mention his desire to improve his lifestyle by seeking a higher-paying position, adopting a more balanced set of priorities, or developing a new group of friends. But economic conditions or social circles have little to do with what the word initially meant to indicate. In the psychological sense, *lifestyle* described one's internal motivations and relationships with people rather than one's external set of circumstances and abundance of possessions.

My associate, Kevin Leman, explains the original thrust of the term this way:

> What exactly is a *lifestyle?* Basically, it is a concept developed by the pioneer psychologist Alfred Adler. Adler believed that understanding a person's goals is a key to understanding a person's behavior. He believed that all of us are following individual "life lines" or paths toward specific goals. Everything we do is oriented toward some goal, whether or not we understand what that goal is. . . .
>
> For the most part, your lifestyle is a product of your environment. It consists of the way you perceive yourself in relationship to the significant people around you. All men and women follow certain lifestyles, which may be either positive or negative. There are the controllers, the pleasers, attention-getters, victims, perfectionists, winners, and so on, all of them following patterns that were established early in life.[1]

Our lifestyle is set early in life and is resistant to change. Telling someone to "snap out of it" when he or she clings to inappropriate attitudes and outlooks is like telling someone who grew up in Spain to stop thinking like a Spaniard at the count of three. Just flying to America won't make you think like an American, nor will a change in social class, marital state, or employment automatically alter your view of life.

And though the spiritual conversion that takes place when we put our trust in Jesus will change our hearts, changing ingrained outlooks can be a daily battle. Paul talks about the ongoing conflict between the old and new natures (see Galatians 5:17). The old nature loves to feed on negative, destructive thought patterns and lifestyles.

LOOKING FOR LIFE THEMES

Human personality is made up of a complex mixture of components. Family environment, birth order, genetics, gender, and other factors play important roles in shaping our life-directing goals and the final product we call personality. There is a constant interplay between the actual father-to-child relationship, the way we remember that relationship, and the emotions we attach to those memories. Therefore, generalizing that certain types of fathering will result in specific lifestyles on the part of a child is overly simplistic.

However, my counseling experience shows that most father memories fall into groups such as the ones I will discuss below. Those categories may help you make sense out of your own memories and the life themes that you have built from them. Although each individual childhood is unique, seeing similarities between your situation and common behavioral tendencies may help you grasp the private logic that is ruling your life, governing your behavior, and interpreting your world.

Father memories are not created equal. Each is as unique as a fingerprint. As you look for consistency in your father memories, check for themes in two specific areas:

- repeated behavior patterns or roles (pleasing, attention seeking, being the black sheep of the family)
- recurring emotional responses to Dad (rejection, encouragement, affirmation, jealousy)

The thread that connects your father memories with your present outlook on life may well run along some of the lines given above. The personality type and leadership style of your father will have an impact on who you are, your response to authority, and your respect for men. Let's look at seven categories into which fathers can fall (and there are others we haven't listed) so that you can get a better idea of where your father fits. Remember, he could easily fall into a combination of categories and carry some characteristics from more than one group.

THE CONTROLLING FATHER

Greg was raised by an extremely authoritarian father, the type I call an offensive controller, someone who manipulates his environment to make others do what he or she wants them to do. Greg's father is a brilliant surgeon on the West Coast and a man accustomed to getting what he wants out of life and others. He always sets his sights high and over the years has expected his children to set their sights high, too.

Never, *can't*, or *won't* are not in his vocabulary. When he sets his mind on something, he refuses to take no for an answer. So compliant son Greg is fearful of getting his knuckles rapped a good one if he dares to tell his father how unenthusiastic he is about pursuing a medical career. Medicine is a family tradition, and Greg knows his dad will perceive his stand as defiance.

"His work always came first" is what Greg remembers most about his father. "All I ever saw in my father was his serious side. We never had fun, and everything seemed to revolve around his work, his patients, his needs. I really don't want the same for myself or my future family, but I feel like I'd be letting my father down if I don't at least give medicine a try."

Although Greg's use of the expressions "never had fun" and "everything revolved around his work" hint at overgeneralization or exaggeration on his part, the description itself indicates that Greg's father has the classic symptoms of a controller. Do you have a controller in your memories? In your present family? Check the statements that are true of you and put a plus mark by those that are true of your father. A controller reasons like this:

- "It's my way or no way."
- "I'm the final authority here, and I have the final word."
- "I like to make things happen and to have them go my way."
- "Everything is set, so don't surprise me. I call the shots."
- "Life is serious and planned out. Don't rock the boat."
- "My opinion is informed and accurate—I'll talk, you listen."

Those statements will sound familiar to an individual raised by a controlling father. A controlling father typically controls everything he touches, including you. That control can take different forms. Some controllers get right to the point and make their positions clear and unchallengeable. Others, like Greg's father, are more subtle. They will bribe, coax, manipulate through guilt, or withhold approval to insure that others behave the way they want them to.

It is true that it is healthy, desirable, and biblical for a child to be raised under the father's authority. But that use of biblically mandated authority to train the child is different from an excessive need to run the child's life. A controlling father abuses his God-given authority.

If you were raised by a controller you were set up for unique problems. In order to maintain some control over your life you may have become a counter-controller and a rebel. Or you may have elected to maintain control by manipulating others or being overly assertive. More often, however, compliant children of controllers (especially women) become pleasers and are reluctant to take control of their own lives. They grow up to discover that they are still wrestling with some or all of the following emotions:

- "I feel like I don't measure up to what is expected of me."
- "I struggle with a passive-aggressive kind of anger. On the surface I appear controlled, but underneath I am angry."
- "I need to be in control of myself to feel OK."
- "I put others before myself in an unhealthy way and often refuse to express my real feelings."
- "It's hard for me to say no to others. I hate feeling like I've let others down."

If your father was a controller, you will discover one or more of the above themes in your memories. For Greg, being the son of a controller has meant a lifetime of conceding his own desires in favor of living up to his father's expectations. Through a forced smile he recalled, "I remember one day when I was about seven. I really wanted to say no to my father, but I just couldn't. I wanted to go next door and play with my friend and at the same time my father wanted me to help him with some sort of project he was working on in the yard. It wasn't so much that I couldn't have gone next door, but I felt a pressure to do what my father expected of me."

Even though his father's request wasn't out of line, the important thing to notice is that Greg remembers not being comfortable with telling his dad he wanted to play with his friend. A general desire to please Dad is not inappropriate or unhealthy. It becomes unhealthy when the child "just can't say no" even when he could.

Greg still feels that pressure. Anytime he has a desire to do something on his own, the father he carries inside himself quickly fire hoses his great idea. Even if Greg's father never says a word, Greg anticipates his father's negative response and "hears" his father's reaction in his head. Greg has internalized his dad's messages and expectations to the point that though no one may mention those expectations out loud they come to mind automatically and exercise control over his decision making.

Does Greg's reluctance to say no, or his feeling of constantly being under his father's thumb, sound like you? Does your dad fit the controller role? Can you hear controller themes when you tell your father memories?

THE DISTANT FATHER

The distant father comes in many varieties. Some distant fathers are dads who traveled frequently, worked long hours, were preoccupied with pressing problems, or were separated from their kids through divorce. Other fathers were emotionally distant and never developed deep bonds with their children. Both physical and emotional distance leave an indelible mark on a child. Most often a child experiences the absence of a father as rejection. He reasons that he or she is not worth his dad's time and attention. Children who grow up in a home with a distant father often have trouble bonding deeply with others or establishing lasting relationships.

Heather's father was around physically, but he might as well not have been as far as she was concerned. His presence did little to meet her need for a father. When she looked into his eyes nobody was home. When he came home at night he took off his coveralls in the back hall, grunted out a greeting of sorts to his wife, and collapsed into his waiting Lazy Boy®. Once there it took a crowbar or an offer of dinner to get him up. Night after night Sam lost himself in the paper or a never-ending round of TV programs.

The message "stay away, please" came through to Heather loud and clear.

Heather recalls, "In all my years at home, I can't remember a single display of affection or tender moment between my parents. My father never hugged or kissed me either." A loving touch, meaningful hug, or even a peck on the cheek were absent. Heather seldom saw her father express *any* emotion. Heather came to believe the message her father was sending—*you are really not that important to me.*

Other life scripts passed from father to daughter:

- "Work is more important than relationships."
- "Children are to be seen and not heard."
- "What I do isn't that important."
- "What I feel isn't that important either."
- "Don't wait for a man to meet your needs."

Heather recalled that as a little girl whenever she wanted to talk to her father he told her her he was busy and asked her to come back later. Heather learned quickly that "later" never happened. As a result, Heather was conditioned to believe lies about life.

- "I need attention so badly that I'll get it any place I can." Women in this environment tend to pick a loser for marriage. They reason that any man will do. They quickly learn that just isn't so.
- "If I just try harder maybe I'll be accepted." Some people will spend a lifetime trying to break through the artificial barrier of acceptance. Those of us with distant fathers pick up the AVIS complex—we try harder.
- "I crave closeness and love, but am afraid of or uncomfortable with intimacy." These individuals often keep their distance or back away from relationships if they grow too close for comfort.

THE WORKAHOLIC FATHER

The workaholic father, like the emotionally distant father, puts work and things before people and emotions. His children grow up conditioned to think that work is the essence of life and often push themselves to unreasonable limits to achieve in order to gain the attention they need.

On the other hand, some children of workaholic fathers conclude that father doesn't know best. They rebel against the never-ending workload that saps all time and energy but leaves one emotionally undernourished. "What's the use," they reason. "It's all a selfish, empty, ego-stroking escape from the responsibility to love one another. When you work all the time there's no time to really get to know anyone or serve anyone except the business."

THE ENCOURAGING FATHER

Psychologist David Semands wrote, "The perceived 'You are's' of the parents become the inner 'I am's' of the children."[2] Children who were raised by encouraging parents have "I am's" that indicate emotional health:

- "I am capable."
- "I am not perfect, but that is OK. I can learn from my mistakes."
- "I am a child of God, and He loves and accepts me as I am."
- "I am able to love and be loved by others. I love and respect myself."
- "It is safe to be open and vulnerable with those I am closest to."

James Dobson, who crusades for strong families as head of the international Christian organization Focus on the Family, was raised by an encouraging father of whom he has spoken often with the warmest affection and respect. Kevin Leman and I had the privilege of being featured for two days on Dr. Dobson's radio broadcast, covering the topic of early childhood memories. While we were on the air, Dr. Dobson told us the first memory he has of his father:

> Let me give you my first recollection of my father, with whom I had a notoriously good relationship, and you tell me what the meaning of it is. This is, I believe, the first time he ever entered into my life that I can recall. It was at the end of the day and my dad,

who was a minister, had been at the church all day. He knocked on the front door instead of coming through it, and I was the one that went and opened the door for him.

When I opened the door, he had a smile on his face as he said, "Come with me." Then he took me around the side of the house and there was a brand new, big, blue tricycle there! It was one exciting moment. As far as surprises of my life, that one probably ranks near the top in terms of sheer delight.[3]

That father memory oozes with love, affection, and tenderness. In Dobson's memory you can sense the importance of the family. Father is seen as a loving, caring, giving parent eager to delight his son. Is it any surprise that the nation's leading advocate for the family would have a father memory like that? It is consistent with how Dobson sees life.

One thing that jumps out in the memory is that he remembers taking responsibility to open the door. The adult James Dobson still takes responsibility. If a door has to be opened, he is going to open it. He's going to be willing to see what's on the other side and deal with it. Another significant phrase is Dobson's comment that his father smiled and said, "Come with me." I contend that those words characterized their relationship overall—they weren't referring just to seeing the new bike. It is also true that the adult James Dobson pictures God as a loving heavenly Father who delights in giving good gifts to His children.

Encouragement is an art. You are a fortunate person if your father memories include the theme of encouragement and loving affirmation. There is no greater legacy a father can leave with his child.

THE CRITICAL FATHER

On the other side of the scale are the critical fathers who just have that look. You know the look I'm talking about—the kind that pierces with disapproval and rejection even if no words are spoken. You could have brought home a report card with four A's and still got the look. The message was "Why the B? This is unacceptable."

Critical fathers can sniff out imperfection from across the room. Joyce grew up with a critical father, as she recalls:

I remember my first day of school. I was so excited to be out with the big kids and finally going to school myself. Mom dressed me up in a cute, fluffy pink dress, handed me a new box of crayons, and deposited me with the kindergarten teacher. I spent the day coloring pictures and playing with the other kids. One of the pictures was of a house with some trees. We were trying to color inside the lines—well I did the best I could.

When I got home that afternoon, I remember that my father was home early but I don't remember why. The part of the memory I recall the clearest is the feeling of rejection after my father looked at my little paper. He looked at it and then at me without a smile or a nod of approval. And he threw my paper on the counter, saying something like "try to be more careful with your work next time." I was crushed.

Joyce is a creative, cautious firstborn. Although her father memory reveals an enjoyment of life, it also shows that she is captive to a fear of criticism. No matter how hard she tries she never thinks that her work is good enough. As she said, "I can't seem to keep inside those lines."

What kind of man do you think Joyce married? If you guessed a "critical Charlie" type, you're right. She goes out of her way to be a pleaser, and if the boat gets rocked, she feels responsible to smooth out the waters.

"Just the other day," Joyce recalls, "I found myself trying to settle an argument between my husband and my son. Then it dawned on me that I wasn't even involved in their problem. I do that a lot."

If you were raised by a critical father, some of the emotional tones listed below probably appear in your memories. Do any of them strike a chord?

- Fear of rejection
- Hurt, humiliation, despondency
- Trying to measure up, but not quite making it
- Feeling picked at or nagged
- Striving for perfection, yet feeling inferior
- Wanting to give up, but knowing you can't

There is a better way to raise children. Contrast the behavior of the critical dads you know with God's instructions for fathers:

"Don't keep on scolding and nagging your children, making them angry and resentful. Rather, bring them up with the loving discipline the Lord himself approves, with suggestions and godly advice" (Ephesians 6:4, TLB*).

THE ANGRY FATHER

The angry father is a one-dimensional man. He responds in anger when other emotions would be more appropriate. When he's tired, disappointed, afraid, insecure, frustrated—you name it—he gets mad. He learned, probably from his own father, that anger gets others to do what you want them to do.

If your father memories are full of anger, you may struggle with these life themes:

- Fear of people
- Feeling alone a lot
- A sense of unpredictability and insecurity
- Overt anger or frozen rage (seen as depression)
- General anxiety
- Doubts about the kindness or goodness of life

The angry father is acting in stark contrast to God's intentions. Our heavenly Father encourages us to "be quick to listen, slow to speak, and slow to become angry, for man's anger does not bring about the righteous life that God desires" (James 1:19-20).

THE ABUSIVE FATHER

The man who is emotionally, sexually, or physically abusive puts his needs before the needs of others. He sees children as objects to be used or as annoyances. Often alcohol or drug dependency is involved, and his children receive mixed messages, depending on whether their father is sober or drunk.

In adults, early father memories of abuse or neglect likewise create a mixture of messages. Research shows that most adults who were abused as children experience some or all of the following feelings or behaviors:

* *The Living Bible.*

- Poor self-concept
- Overly responsible
- Controlling
- Compulsive
- Obsessive
- People pleasers to an unhealthy extreme
- Perfectionistic
- Procrastinator

A WORD OF ENCOURAGEMENT

At this point in our look at fathers some of you are weighted down and discouraged by your father memories. To those of you in that camp, here are a few points of encouragement:

- You can be freed from father memories.
- Permanent change is possible—you can break the cycle.
- God cares about your father memories and your damaged emotions.
- You are not alone—many others feel as you do.
- You can face your felt pain and overcome it.

In *Healing Grace* David Semands offers these suggestions concerning painful memories: "Relive them in your emotions, but don't stop there. Relinquish them to God in forgiving and surrendering prayer. It's doubtful you can do this by yourself, so get help from a close friend, pastor, or counselor."[4] Beyond that, begin today to abandon the lies that hold you captive to your memories by using the techniques that follow in the remainder of this book.

If you were raised by a father who in some way deprived you of the attention, affection, and security you needed, looking back will not be easy. Please stay with me, even if you feel an aching emptiness or terror or rage when you look back at your childhood. The next few chapters of this book focus on healthy ways to fill the father-void and how to exchange negative life themes and expectations for a positive, healthy outlook.

Notes

1. Kevin Leman, *Measuring Up* (New York: Revell, 1988), pp. 13-14. Information based on Alfred Adler, *The Practice of Individual Psychology* (London: Routeledge & Kegan Paul, 1923), p. 3.
2. David A. Semands, *Healing Grace* (Wheaton, Ill.: Victor, 1988), p. 153.
3. James Dobson as heard on the "Focus on the Family" broadcast, August 1989.
4. Semands, *Healing Grace,* p. 162.

5

So Dad Dropped the Ball

In Jackie Gleason's biography *How Sweet It Is,* we learn that the childhood of this successful comedian and actor was far from sweet. Both his father and mother drank heavily, and even in his preschool days Jackie remembers putting his mother to bed when she was tipsy.[1] "I was about nine when one day my pop didn't come home," Gleason recalls. "A few days before, my mom and he had a violent argument and he took every picture out of the house that had him in it. That should have been the tip-off, but I was too young to know."[2] Jackie never saw his dad again. His father's sudden departure left the Gleason family destitute, and the tragedy had a visible effect on Jackie—it left him with an appetite bordering on gluttony that hounded him until death.

Even so, as an adult Jackie Gleason chose to cast his father in a benevolent light:

> I remember thinking when they first told me he had died, if he had only dropped by once to say hello. Surely, he must have seen me on TV. Everybody else in the country did. I never was angry about Pop leaving us. I figured there must be something between him and Mom that I didn't know about. He always was okay with me. He had a great sense of humor, that I do remember. If he had just dropped by once. Just once.[3]

From his father memory we get a clear picture of how the adult Jackie Gleason viewed his father. He chose to see his father as

- a victim of circumstances
- an OK father—even though he wasn't around
- passing on a good inheritance—a great sense of humor
- a missing piece of his life he could never find but longed for

How Sweet It Is—Or Isn't

Gleason's life could have gone in a different direction if he had chosen to wallow in the emotional pain and poverty of his past. Instead, Gleason chose to accept his circumstances and make the most of his abilities. Notice how far removed his reasoning is from the private logic of those who assume a victim lifestyle. Victims reason something like this:

- I AM surely the most unfortunate of human beings.
- OTHER PEOPLE ARE going to have to take pity and make allowances for my terrible plight.
- THE WORLD is surely out to get me, and it's succeeding.[4]

Meeting new friends at a live father-memory seminar is a high point of my work. I get a thrill out of helping others—so much so that I'll stand for an hour or two after a seminar has ended to help just one person make sense of his past. Even when I'm so tired I can hardly put words together in a sentence, I'll be there. I don't say this with pride, for I'm learning how easily we can do good things for the wrong reasons.

As you know from reading just a few of my father memories, I don't want anybody to go home from a seminar unhappy or with a question left unanswered. I've told myself the lie, "I'm responsible to fix other people's problems."

My motive for helping is right, but my sense of responsibility is wrong. That kind of thinking gets me into trouble and out of balance. I'm thankful for my wife, Donna, who has learned how to gently help me challenge my thinking. She reminds me that I can't change anyone else or improve his life—he alone must make any changes that are made. I can provide information, encouragement, and prayer support, but I can't be responsible for what he does with what I give him—and it is not *his* problem if I don't reserve enough time for my family. I am not the victim, on call without choice every time someone has a need.

In our clear-thinking moments most of us realize that the world is not out to get us and that we are often our own worst enemies. We talk ourselves into overcommitment, make poor decisions, yield to sinful behavior, or fail to exercise self-control, and, as a consequence, we end up in difficult circumstances—or in the same old situation with the same old problems.

Regardless of your childhood and early relationship with your father, you still have choices. You can make the most of life, as Jackie Gleason chose to, and find a better life starting today. To do so you will need to cast your memories in a positive light and choose to focus on the best in yourself and others. That doesn't mean that you deny reality, only that you elect to play to your strengths and compensate for weak areas in your upbringing.

We Can Like Ourselves Even Without Being Perfect

I still cringe inwardly at one of my earliest memories. I misspelled a one-syllable word during a school spelling bee and even to this day remember how dumb and embarrassed I felt. Everybody laughed. (And I'm not going to mention what the word was, or you will chuckle, too!) When I think of that incident I vividly recall the setting of the room, the teacher's face, and my own emotions. And I find myself thinking, *How could you be so stupid to have misspelled such a simple word?* But I stop myself short.

Why? Because I know that most of what I tell myself from my early memories is at best a half-truth, at worst a lie. The truth is, I didn't like spelling and therefore didn't spend much time in preparation. I'm not stupid. You're not either. As you look at your memories, give yourself and your father the right to make mistakes and to fail. Though you cannot change the *content* of the memory, you can change the *context* in which you interpret it. And you can change the message you tell yourself based upon that incident.

You can like yourself without being perfect. Don't exaggerate your flaws or failures.

My wife and I were invited to have dinner with some friends in their home. When we arrived, the couple had a wonderful meal ready and the husband, Eric, was putting the finishing touches on some barbecued chicken on the grill. His wife, Cathy, immediately began a string of half-joking apologies: "I'm really a horrible cook, so don't expect too much. Eric agreed to do the chicken and the potatoes, so you won't starve."

Our friend Cathy would be an excellent candidate for truth therapy. A large serving of truth would do wonders for her home life. And the truth is that though she may be an average cook, she certainly doesn't qualify as a "horrible" one. One look at her healthy, active family confirms that they eat well. Her all-or-nothing outlook distorts her perception.

It is also true that Cathy is an extremely gifted, intelligent woman and has a beautiful soprano voice. She doesn't need to put herself down because cooking isn't her thing. Our culture reinforces the message that it's not OK for a woman to be an average cook—or an average anything! Baby boomers are supposed to be excellent at everything they do—even though we each have average abilities in many areas and get along just fine.

Cathy, like all of us, does things without knowing their source. She needs to remember that our behavior begins in our minds. Here's the principle:

Thinking precedes behavior and emotions.

Every action began as an idea; every reaction began with judgment about the trigger event. What you think dictates your behavior and emotional response. Cathy's feelings about herself and the patterns that govern her thought life did not take shape in a vacuum. The little girl she once was made conclusions based upon her early experiences and formed a private logic to make sense of her world. As an adult, Cathy needs to upgrade her inner programming.

Parenting the Little Child Inside

Because Cathy's father died when she was three and her mother turned to alcohol to cope, Cathy has no memory of encouraging words from her parents. But Cathy, and all children, needed huge doses of encouragements like these:

"You did it all by yourself—great!"
"I can see you worked hard on that!"
"Do that again!"
"I have faith in you!"
"That's good thinking!"
"That's a terrific paper—let's put it up on the refrigerator."
"I appreciate what you've done!"

Part of Cathy's therapy should include catching herself whenever she mentally or verbally puts herself down and replacing that thought with a positive affirmation similar to the statements above. The adult Cathy will need to discipline her thought life and nurture the encouragement-starved little girl inside. It will also help, of course, for Cathy to surround herself with positive, supportive friends who will assist in the process. And she would be wise to avoid critical friends or acquaintances who focus on comparisons.

Cathy should also take an honest look at why she berates herself in front of close friends and family members. She needs to ask herself: Do I really accept these negative views of myself? Or when I say negative things about myself am I really fishing for reassurance and compliments, baiting my friends with a negative remark so that they will meet my need for encouragement and prop up my self-esteem? Am I taking a helpless little girl stance in my marriage so that my husband will step in as the teaching, caring, affirming father figure I never had?

Self-parenting should always be done gently, privately, and without fanfare. This is no time for abrupt, harsh, self-talk: "There I go again, making those same stupid mistakes! I shouldn't have said that . . . I shouldn't have done this . . ." Never privately rehearse your mistakes or publicly draw attention to your weaknesses. Instead, constantly renew your mind with God's perspective of your value, uniqueness, and significance as a person and think on those things that are positive and true. That leads to an important principle:

> The key to permanent change is to have an accurate view of who you really are and your true potential. Refuse to believe or live out those lies that have become ingrained in your lifestyle.

That is easier said than done. Whenever I autograph a book I make reference to one of the most meaningful verses in the Bible. It has been a challenge toward a new way of thinking for me: "Fix your thoughts on what is true and good and right. Think about things that are pure and lovely, and dwell on the fine, good things in others. Think about all you can praise God for and be glad about (Philippians 4:8, TLB)." The verse relates to focusing one's mind upon God and His truth and beauty and then disciplining ourselves to dwell on constructive thoughts and truth.

YOUR PAST TOUCHES OTHER PEOPLE

You need to change any destructive messages you live by not only for your sake but for the sake of your loved ones. The lies you tell yourself from your father memories and your emotions and behavior affect other people, especially the people you love and who love you.

William and Candace Backus, authors of *What Did I Do Wrong? What Can I Do Now?*, call destructive inner messages *radical misbelief.* They define radical misbelief as "a strongly held erroneous belief upon which you base your view of yourself and others."[5] Radical misbeliefs lead to all sorts of faulty thinking about relationships and life. Here are some misbelief statements I've heard flow out of father memories. Put a check mark by any you may have caught yourself thinking:

_____ "I don't deserve my children. I'm a bad parent."

_____ "If I don't measure up to my spouse's expectations it will be awful."

_____ "My child has run away from home (misbehaved, rebelled, whatever). It must be all my fault."

_____ "To be a good employee I need to work at least an hour a day longer than everyone else."

_____ "A good Christian would never say no or refuse to help."

_____ "God loves me less because of what I've done."

_____ "Nobody cares what happens to me. The world would be better off if I were dead."

Lies like that come straight from Satan, the father of lies. Don't believe a word of them! Take a hard look at any misbeliefs from your father memories that may be damaging your relationships today or ruining your life. God has the power to help you overcome lies with truth.

CHANGING YOUR PERCEPTION OF THE PAST

With God's help, you can change your perception of the past by rewriting your memories and the feelings attached to them. Challenge the perceptions you had as a child, and which are now frozen in your memory, and replace them with the rational thinking you are capable of as an adult. As you gain a proper perspective on your memories, you can change your self-talk. And when you change your self-talk—how you think all day long—you can change your behavior.

On our radio call-in program, "Parent Talk," Kevin Leman and I discussed Jane's father memory and explained how she could rewrite it. Here is the father memory Jane had recounted:

> As a very little girl, I was walking hand in hand with my father through the woods behind our cabin. I clearly remember looking up at Dad and the trees and thinking how big my dad was and how tall all the trees were—it was kind of scary to be so small. I was glad Dad was with me.

As an adult, Jane was still feeling small and insignificant in a big, big world. She agreed that the father memory echoed her current desire to have someone "hold her hand" through major projects. She still looked up to Dad and pictured herself as dependent upon his help.

Jane's father memory has many positive qualities: the warmth and affection of walking hand in hand; the special attention of time alone with Dad; and having a protective, caring father. I encouraged Jane to go back through the memory as an adult and change her perception. As a woman Jane could see that the little girl was loved and cared for—she did not need to feel afraid or inadequate. Her father was pleased to spend time with her, not concerned that she didn't measure up. She was imagining her shortcomings.

Specifically, I encouraged Jane to mentally visualize herself taking the same walk with her father as an adult and enjoying one another's companionship as adult friends. Jane went one step further and actually revisited the cabin and took the same walk with her father. "It's amazing how the trees have shrunk!" she later remarked. That little trip down memory lane opened the door for Jane to begin believing in herself as a capable, contributing adult. Although she still admires and loves her father, she no longer feels small and dependent without him.

You Deserve a Break Today!

It is easy to look at ourselves and our past through binoculars that magnify our problems, hurts, and faults. But when we search for positive characteristics we sometimes flip the binoculars around and shrink the successes and the positive aspects of our past and our personality. If you find that is true of you, throw away the warped lens and look straight at life. You deserve a break!

Bill has three well-adjusted children and eight delightful grandchildren. At age sixty-five, he has had what many would call a successful life. But when you talk to Bill about his life, he quickly focuses on what he calls "the lost years." His conversation always comes back to his regrets: "I was too harsh with my kids when they were young. I also worked too much and missed out on time with them."

One day I asked Bill if he ever thought about the flip side of his memories of fathering and considered what the flip side said about him as a man and a father. "Bill, there's more to that story than the empty page," I told him. "Look at your kids today—they're doing great. You gave them boundaries, love, and discipline. You weren't perfect. No father is. But isn't it time to look at the good and focus on all you've done right?"

How do you see yourself? Picky? Stingy? Wishy-washy? Many times the negative traits we recognize are highly exaggerated. Other times the self-defeating aspects of our personality we adopt as part of our lifestyle are positive qualities misused. A change in perspective and a healthy dose of self-control will bring them back into focus.

Conversely, our strengths often have a flip side of weakness. That is, when we carry a good thing to the extreme it can become undesirable, or a negative behavior may actually be prompted by a commendable motivation improperly carried out. So if you don't see strengths or positive characteristics in yourself or your memories at first glance, don't be discouraged. There are some strengths hidden there that you can build upon.

John remembers several instances of friction with his father that came about because of his own stubbornness. Pretty negative stuff. Yet as an adult, John has succeeded in establishing a business by overcoming tremendous obstacles that would have defeated a less determined man. Resisting everyone who claimed it couldn't be done, he hung onto his dream and worked to achieve it. In this case, the personality quality of the little boy matured with the man—stubbornness was determination in disguise.

Brent came into my office feeling like a total failure as a father. "I told myself I would never do what my dad did. But now I find myself repeating many of the very same mistakes," he reported. Specifically, Brent was troubled by his impatience and irritability with his little girl. When I asked Brent to tell about the things he was doing right as a father, and his personal strengths, he couldn't come up with anything positive. But as we talked it became evident that Brent's strong point—and his downfall—was his sensitivity. Brent was of such a nature as to be easily affected by emotions and to have powerful feelings in response to others and events. Brent couldn't change his underlying personality, but he didn't need to apologize for it or let it ruin his relationships either.

I encouraged Brent to express his sensitivity openly when it prompted constructive emotions such as compassion, understanding, and excitement over the successes his little girl experienced. But when his powerful feelings tended toward overreaction or irritability, I suggested that he delay his response until he had his feelings more in balance. He needed to learn to channel his strong feelings into appropriate outlets. "I know I do better at exercising self-control when I'm not in a hurry. And I'm more patient on days when I get enough sleep, avoid caffeine, and take time to work out," Brent admitted. Then he grinned and added, "But most days I don't feel like doing all that!"

So what else is new? The little child in *all* of us resists doing "all those things" that adults are expected to do. And when the little child inside rules the roost, look out! The result is immaturity and selfish behavior. When our adult better judgment yields to the childish side of our nature that wants what we want when we want it, our personality strengths and abilities become defects. But, like Brent, we can still put our strong points to good use when we choose to.

The chart on pages 80-81 lists many character qualities you may attach to the little child in your father memories and also to your character today. In the first column are the positive attributes. In the second column are descriptions of positive qualities misused, which show themselves as negative traits. Try to identify two or three main traits in your personality. Then list two ways you can make the positive aspect of those traits work for you more effectively in your present relationships.

WHAT YOU SEE IS WHAT YOU GET

The mind is a powerful tool for shaping our lives. There is a self-fulfilling element to the way we visualize our future and mentally see ourselves. The brain, both consciously and subconsciously, seeks to carry out the instructions it has been given. Thus if you mentally replay statements such as, "I am creative and good at solving problems," or, "With God's help I'm going to get through this," or any positive directive, your mind will follow up on the self-suggestion.

Most of us, however, need to work hard at reprogramming negative, inaccurate lies we picked up in childhood. In order to take control of our lives, we need to control our thoughts and constantly screen them against the truth. Take a moment now to try to list three misbeliefs or negative life themes that are evident in your early memories and in your life today. Then rewrite those statements according to the truth and determine your strategy for altering your behavior in light of what you know to be true.

For example, as a cautious and careful man, I have to overcome my reluctance to take risks by reminding myself of the truth: It's OK to take calculated risks. The business decisions I encounter daily involve weighing cost to benefit and benefit to risk, then making good judgments based on experience. My strategy for not letting negative misbeliefs take over is simply *to stop and think*. I want to be aware of times when my temperament may be influencing my decisions, and so I ask myself: *Is this a risk I'm willing to take to achieve these benefits? Or am I avoiding this situation just because it's unfamiliar and involves some risk? Am I just playing it safe and trying to please others rather than making what I believe to be the best choice?*

I hate spending money. Just ask my wife. So you can imagine my frustration as the president of a growing radio, seminar, and counseling business. In business, spending money is a way of life. Even so, I identify more with the saying "A penny saved is a penny earned" than the saying "You have to spend money to make money." But I'm learning that both approaches have their merit.

Recently the work load got so demanding that I decided to hire two new full-time people to work directly for me. It was a matter of emotional and physical survival. But before I hired them I had to reason with myself to come to the place where I could accept the truth—I needed more help, and the new employees would help the business grow. I acted on that truth, even though it went against my natural response to the situation. My reluctance to spend money had to be overruled by truth in the decision-making process. That's good for me. That's good for business.

Heidi was held back by a different sort of logic from her childhood. She had an ingrained achievement-oriented approach to life. Her father memories revealed several different occasions where she had received love, attention, and praise for a job well done. Heidi's strong desire to please had led to a distorted outlook on the proper value of performance. She had concluded—falsely— that she needed to earn the approval and affection of others.

In order to take the air out of her inflated father memories, I asked Heidi to restate the positive aspect of her father's response to her: "Dad was interested in my life. He encouraged me to do my best. He affirmed my best efforts and would not accept sloppy work." Then she went to work on the lies that had become part of her lifestyle. In completing the exercise below, Heidi wrote, "From childhood I have been acting out the belief that my work determines my worth. But the truth is, I don't have to earn my acceptance by working hard. I am a valuable person apart from my performance."

Positive Quality (Desirable Traits)	Positive Quality Misused (Negative Traits)
Alert, aware	Jumpy, wary, on guard
Amiable, friendly	Charmer, socialite, spineless
Analytical	Picky, calculating, crabby, petty
Aspiring, ambitious	Overambitious, competitive, scheming
Compassionate	Overly sentimental, gushy, undue pity
Confident	Overconfident, conceited, overbearing
Cooperative	Compromising, peer-influenced, conspiring
Courageous	Reckless, brash
Courteous	Superficial, polite to a fault
Creative	Crafty, mischievous, day-dreaming
Curious	Snoopy, nosy, scrutinizing
Decisive	Domineering, inflexible, controlling
Diligent	One-track-mind, overconscientious
Discerning	Judgmental, critical, fault-finding
Disciplined	Inflexible, harsh, tyrannical
Discreet, diplomatic	Secretive, shifty, manipulative
Earnest	Meticulous, overly serious, stick-in-the mud
Efficient	Impatient, fussy, overly organized
Enthusiastic	Fanatical, dramatic, overbearing
Expressive	Wordy, glib, nonstop talker
Flexible	Wishy-washy, indecisive, uncommitted
Forgiving	Lenient, condoning, push-over
Frank	Tactless, insensitive
Frugal	Stingy, tightwad, penny-pincher
Fun-loving	Irresponsible, impulsive
Generous	Financially irresponsible, wasteful
Grateful	Flattering, gushy, indebted, pleasing

Positive Quality (Desirable Traits)	Positive Quality Misused (Negative Traits)
Honest, open	Outspoken, blunt, too revealing
Humble	Unassertive, self-abasement
Loyal	Possessive, clingy, covering for others
Neat	Overparticular, perfectionistic
Obedient, submissive	Overly compliant, doormat type
Objective, rational	Cold, unfeeling, detached
Patient	Indifferent, permissive
Persistent	Stubborn, headstrong, relentless
Persuasive	Pushy, smooth talker, manipulative
Punctual	Intolerant of tardiness, rigid
Purposeful, determined	Driven, inflexible, unyielding
Respectful	Intimidated, worshiping
Resolute, committed	Closed-minded, hardheaded
Resourceful	Overly self-reliant, clever, shrewd
Sensitive	Touchy, easily offended, reactive, moody
Sincere	Holier-than-thou, naive
Spontaneous	Slipshod, disorganized, impulsive
Talented, capable	Superior, self-centered, lofty
Thoughtful	Solicitous, worried what others think
Understanding	Indulgent, overly empathetic
Virtuous, noble-minded	High-minded, goody-two-shoes
Wise, insightful	Know-it-all, bossy, self-assured

Now you try the exercise with the most important distortion of the truth you've been reciting all these years. Complete the following sentences:

From childhood I have been acting out the belief that _____

_____

_____

But the truth is _____

_____

If your father died or was absent for other reasons during your formative years, you may have many self-talk statements that need to be challenged. In the next chapter we will discuss some effective strategies to counter the effects of poor fathering or to fill a father-void.

Notes

1. James Bacon, *How Sweet It Is: The Jackie Gleason Story* (New York: St. Martin's, 1985), p. 5.
2. Ibid., p. 6.
3. Ibid., p. 9.
4. Randy Carlson and Kevin Leman, *Unlocking the Secrets of Your Childhood Memories* (Nashville: Thomas Nelson, 1989), p. 80.
5. William and Candace Backus, *What Did I Do Wrong? What Can I Do Now?* (Minneapolis: Bethany, 1990), p. 40.

6

FILLING THE FATHER VOID

If you missed out on a father's love, you missed a lot. Although there are ways to compensate for the lack of a father's involvement, making positive father memories from the very first is far superior than making up for a lack of them later on.

My parents founded Youth Haven Ranch camps for underprivileged children, and my brother, Larry, and his wife now manage the youth ministry. Around four thousand kids, many from the inner city, go through the program each year. Through this experience, our family has had numerous opportunities to observe the effects of a father's abandonment, rejection, abuse, neglect, or addictions. Many of the youngsters at the camps would be hardpressed to come up with a single happy father memory.

Larry has worked closely with boys and girls who come from troubled homes, and he has seen them search for a father figure to fill their need for attention, love, and significance. Larry's observation based upon his youth camp experience echoes my conclusion based upon counseling experience. We agree that:

> Every child will search out something or someone in the flesh to fill the father void—sometimes inappropriately.

Every child will seek to fill the longing for a father's love in a relationship with someone or something in this world. Some children will find constructive strategies to compensate. Other children will be drawn to inappropriate and ultimately self-destructive ways of coping with their father void.

As a counselor, I have come to see that the search my brother speaks of is often a never-ending longing. The father-deprived boy or girl may experience that emptiness long into adulthood—the need for a stable father image does not magically disappear as one grows older. Nor is the emotional need automatically met by a spiritual relationship with God, our Father in heaven.

When Dad Didn't Meet Your Emotional Needs

Some of you reading this book cringe at the thought of your childhood relationship or lack of interaction with your father. Others long for a closer bond with Dad, but that relationship appears destined not to be. What can you do right now, as an adult, if your dad didn't meet your emotional needs in the past? How can you change your course of life if your childhood relationship with your father preconditioned you toward disappointment and failure? How can you feel whole and healthy if there were gaps in the nurturing and training that were part of your upbringing?

MENTORS AND OTHER AUTHORITY FIGURES CAN HELP TO FILL THE GAP

First, you need to recognize how deeply the need for affirmation and affection from a father figure influences your present relationships. Second, you need to seek socially and morally acceptable ways to fill those emotional needs yet at the same time come to terms with your less-than-ideal past.

One step you can take is to build relationships with caring men from your church who can offer fatherly advice and emotional support. Civic groups, business networks, or health clubs may also provide opportunities to build relationships with men who can serve as examples and mentors. Be careful, however, not to set yourself up for disappointment with unrealistic expectations or unreasonable time demands.

If you are a man who has much to offer a needy child or young adult, get involved on the giving end. "I've had the opportunity to become a surrogate father for several kids, even into adulthood," my brother explains. "Next week I'll be walking one young woman down the aisle, standing in for the father she has never known. She knows I care about her, and I'm always available if she needs advice or someone to talk to." Men like Larry serve as important role models in helping young men and women establish stable, loving homes and purposeful lives.

Paul, a thirty-four-year-old computer analyst, found help through the mentoring relationship with a senior engineer at the company where he worked. "I really admired and respected Jerry and was pleased when he took an interest in me—even though looking back I can see that he had to intervene before I destroyed the morale in his department!" Paul reported with a grin. "Through Jerry's example in handling his own work load and his helpful insights into management concerns, I saw problems in my own behavior and made some changes. I learned new work habits and constructive attitudes—things my own father never had time to teach me."

"The funny thing is, even though Jerry and I never discussed my home life, I became more involved in shepherding my son through routine tasks and repair projects," Paul adds. "When Jerry dove into my problems at work he made all kinds of ripples in the water! The best thing I ever did was to listen to Jerry."

Jerry's impact as a mentor was far-reaching. His actions demonstrate the wisdom of the biblical exhortation for older men to encourage younger men to be self-controlled and "in everything set them an example by doing what is good" (Titus 2:7).

Unfortunately, we have nearly lost the art of mentoring or apprenticeship in our culture. Our fragmented society has left many individuals stranded at both extremes of the relationship scale. An overemphasis on independence has left some people in the gutter of isolation, and unhealthy dependence has left others in the gutter of codependence. Both are bad news.

Where do you look for a good example? There is a natural tendency to project the father role onto those in positions of authority. You may find yourself looking toward your boss, your pastor, or your family physician as a father figure. Although any of those bonds may be healthy and satisfying, the search for someone to fill an emotional emptiness can lead to improper behavior or illicit relationships. Women, especially, need to beware of their desire for attachment and support from men.

Make sure you really get to understand the person and his motives fully before divulging personal problems. Before you invest yourself in a mentoring-type friendship with another person, examine his character and personal qualities:

1. *Look for someone who is a good role model and person of integrity.* Friends rub off on us in many ways. Values and beliefs are important, and theirs should be in most cases more solid and tested than ours.
2. *Look for someone who will be honest with you and who seeks accountability.* People who only tell you what you want to hear aren't real friends. It takes iron to sharpen iron—and sometimes the result makes for a few sparks.
3. *Look for someone who will set and maintain healthy boundaries with regard to how much help to give.* The goal in the relationship is to develop a healthy interdependence, not a dependent or codependent relationship.
4. *For your closest friendships, chose someone of the same sex, even if you long for a father figure.* Every woman should be warned that many relationships with an older man that began innocently with a little fatherly advice developed eventually into immoral sexual involvement. Be sure healthy hedges are in place.

SEX IS NOT A HEALTHY SUBSTITUTE

Ann's father was killed in a truck accident when she was six. In junior high she became close friends with her coach and turned to him for help with her personal problems. By the time she reached high school, little Ann had blossomed into an attractive young woman and the intimate friendship with her coach grew into an affair. "Deep down I knew he would never leave his family to marry me, but that didn't matter at the time," Ann recalls. "I was so starved for masculine attention that I was willing to give sex to get love. Instead I got used—and hurt. When he suddenly dropped out of my life I kept asking silently through my sobs, 'Why do the men I love always leave me?'"

A destructive pattern was set, and Ann's memory of her father's abruptly leaving her family became a haunting, self-fulfilling prophecy. In my counseling experience I've seen similar situations repeated often—the intense experience of abandonment, rejection, or abuse are adopted as life themes and repeated. So I give this warning to women: *never* seek to fill your need for fatherly protection, care, love, and companionship through any relationship involving sexual intimacy. Even within the marriage bond, the relationship should be kept on an adult-to-adult, not parent-child, level. The warning also applies to men: don't look to homosexual relationships to fill your father void.

GODLY ROLE MODELS

Your goal is to build right, moral, good, and healthy friendships with older men of good reputation. Seek role models—possibly an uncle, grandfather, or father-in-law—who can affirm you and train you by example in how to father your children and re-parent yourself. That way the negative cycle will be broken in your generation.

Mark was raised in a Christian home by a faithful father who took his parenting responsibilities seriously but remained emotionally distant from his sons. "Shortly after I married Judy I began to realize what a special gift God had given me through my relationship with Judy's father," Mark said. "He has affirmed my masculinity in new areas and communicated acceptance of me in a way I've never experienced with my own dad. He frequently says things like, 'You're doing a great job playing with the boys—they'll have great memories of your times together,' or, 'I'm proud of you, Mark!' My father-in-law has given me the chance to enjoy a loving, open relationship within the intimate family structure. He has taught me tenderness."

Many times older men have learned through their mistakes and can pass on the benefit of their experience. As time passes, we may be seeking healthy role models for our own children and be doubly blessed by our contact with men we look up to.

In this way Sally, a struggling single parent with no close relatives, found a rewarding cross-generational relationship when an elderly couple from her church befriended her children. As Sally's children spent time with their adopted grandparents, Sally benefited from the couple's wisdom and emotional support. The relationship was an example of the church family operating at its best.

Sally had no memories of fatherly care and no capacity to feel tenderness toward God as a father. But as she experienced the warm support the couple offered, she felt a deep sense of belonging and being loved for the first time. That, in turn, deepened her relationship with God and became the model for her own parenting. We hear a lot these days about dysfunctional cycles, but healthy and whole parenting styles can also be spawned.

LOVE AND WORK

My dad remembers one group of young campers who spent most of their time on the basketball court. He called them over for a snack, but one boy, Isiah, stayed on the court shooting hoops. Later he called the campers over for another activity, but Isiah lingered, taking more jump shots. So my father walked over to him, put his arm around his shoulder and said, "You know, Isiah, there's more to life than basketball."

My father was right, there is more to life than basketball, but for Isiah Thomas basketball was the road to a happier, more successful life. And Isiah poured his whole heart into the pursuit of excellence on the court and became an impressive professional in the NBA.

Setting and achieving worthy goals can make you feel better about yourself, regardless of your background. Living life with a purpose can help to fill the emptiness you sense in your father memories.

A healthy, fulfilled life is generally balanced on twin pillars: *love* and *work*. Each of us needs to feel loved and accepted. We have a need for significance, too—a need to know that our efforts and our presence are important to someone, a need to be somebody. Being accepted in the workplace and feeling good about our contributions to the world and the work of our hands can take the edge off of a painful past. As one woman put it, "If you want to feel good about yourself, do something you can feel good about!"

In the Bible God lays down a principle, "Say to the righteous that it will go well with them, for they will eat the fruit of their actions" (Isaiah 3:10, NASB*). There is a satisfying, filling sense of well-being that comes as a result of living rightly and doing good.

* *New American Standard Bible.*

Many people begin to fill the father void with the satisfaction that comes from obedient living, meaningful work, worthy achievement, or skillful performance. That puts them in a stronger position to deal with negative prior father memories.

The quest for success can be be taken to unhealthy extremes, however. The relentless pursuit of money, work, things, success, power, excellence, flawless appearance—or any other material aspect of life—cannot ultimately satisfy your deepest needs.

Workaholism can become a means to escape damaged relationships and avoid being hurt or rejected again. Money can begin to look like the answer to your problems. Yet materialism will not heal the deep wounds caused by a father's rejection, absence, or abuse. History books are packed with stories of men such as Howard Hughes, who experienced financial success, power, and fame but failed to establish lasting, loving relationships with God and with other people. It is important to keep performance and success in their proper perspective.

Frank was about to die and wanted one final meeting with his family. He had started his career with a ten dollar bill and had built that small sum into a thriving business empire, having little time for family or friends. Now, on his deathbed, you might expect that he would have a repentant heart and a changed attitude. No way. All Frank knew was how to make money and run his business. When the family gathered around he had only one request: "Put a ten dollar bill in my hand before they close the coffin so I can start another business on the other side."

Sad but true. Frank devoted his whole life to an empty pursuit, making money his god.

Your goal is to seek a proper balance, loving deeply as well as working hard. Hard work is healthy. Satisfying, productive labor instills in you a sense of purpose and significance. Self-discipline leads to emotional health. Lazy individuals rarely work through the bad habits or hurts from their past to achieve a healthy, productive balance in life. As it says in the book of Proverbs, "All hard work brings a profit" (14:23).

Doing good work and receiving positive feedback will help you develop a strong self-image. It will bring out ingrained talents and abilities. The more you can see yourself becoming what you want to be, the more your present fulfillment will override your father void.

That will have a practical application. Are you depressed about your past? Get up, take a shower, and go to work anyway. Or take a long, brisk walk. Depression and chemical reactions in the brain go hand in hand. If you think and act depressed long enough your brain starts to believe it, and chemical changes occur. In some cases the chemical changes bring on the depression. But in either case, physical exercise will elevate the level of endorphins (good chemicals) in the brain and help restore balance. So depression generally subsides as the level of physical activity increases.

Laughter also activates the release of endorphins. Cultivating a good sense of humor can help to bring on feelings of well-being and inner peace.

If you feel empty because you have never known a father's love, work at being the loving, involved parent you longed for in your own child's life. Be there for a troubled child in the same way you wish someone had stepped alongside to help you. In giving you will receive, and you will enjoy the fruit of your labor. Satisfaction lies in seeing results. You say you don't like your memories? Work at making good ones.

And work at building a strong relationship with your Father in heaven.

LOVE AND AFFECTION FROM YOUR FATHER IN HEAVEN

At Youth Haven Ranch camps my family attempts to direct children to the One who can satisfy their innermost needs. We are well aware, however, that a child's relationship with his or her earthly father colors the way he sees his heavenly Father. As my brother Larry remarked in a recent conversation, "For father-deprived children God is often irrelevant. Their private logic says, 'God has abandoned me.' Or they see God as detached and unconcerned about them and reason that they can't depend on Him or trust Him to come through for them. They project their own emotional profile—if you don't have a good father image you won't have a good God-father image."

These children, as well as children from strong families, carry the image they have of their father into adulthood, seeing God through the same set of glasses their daddy gave them. Counselor

Norman Wright explains, "One of the main reasons people hold false perceptions of God is their tendency to project onto God the unloving characteristics of the people we look up to."[1]

Wanda, for example, was raised by a father who broke his promises, left for days at a time without notice, and seldom considered Wanda's needs. Believing that God cared about her, would answer her prayers, and always kept His promises was hard for her. Wanda had to memorize many verses about God's faithfulness and refuse to give in to what she intuitively felt (based upon her father memories) was true of God's character. Wanda was able to interrupt the projecting process, but it took a great deal of effort.

The following inventory, adapted from the book *We Are Driven*,[2] will help you see if your vision of God is tinted by the lens of your father's love and leadership style (or that of the authority figure who raised you). Check the statements below that reflect your vision of God and then substitute for God's name the name of your father or someone who raised you. See if there is a one-to-one correspondence. There won't always be, but many times there is a direct relationship.

1. _____ "I see God as someone who cares personally and intimately for me and my welfare."

   "I see _____ as someone who cares personally and intimately for me and my welfare."

2. _____ "I view God as a source of nonjudgmental and unconditional love."

   "I view _____ as a source of nonjudgmental and unconditional love."

3. _____ "God is someone I can talk openly and freely with about my problems and my needs."

   "_____ is someone I can talk openly and freely with about my problems and my needs."

4. ____ "I trust that God hears and responds to my deepest needs and concerns."

"I trust that _____ hears and responds to my deepest needs and concerns."

5. ____ "I question whether or not God genuinely loves me and accepts me."

"I question whether or not _____ genuinely loves me and accepts me."

6. ____ "I see God as a harsh, stern disciplinarian, and I fear His punishment and wrath."

"I see _____ as a harsh, stern disciplinarian, and I fear his punishment and wrath."

7. ____ "I am angry and bitter at God about past failures or illnesses or disappointments. I wonder why God has not spared me from these."

"I am angry and bitter at _____ about past failures or illnesses or disappointments. I wonder why _____ has not spared me from these."

8. ____ "God seems distant and remote from me."

"_____ seems distant and remote from me."

9. ____ "I imagine God's agenda is so filled with people and things far more important than I. Surely He doesn't notice me."

"I imagine _____'s agenda is so filled with people and things far more important than I. Surely _____ doesn't notice me."

10. _____   "Some part of me feels so unworthy. I question if I could ever win God's love and approval."

"Some part of me feels so unworthy. I question if I could ever win _____'s love and approval."

As an adult you need to be open to another view of God, one that is shaped by the truth of the Bible as it describes God's character, not one shaped by your experiences as a child relating to your father. That will require a directed effort to study, memorize, and apply Scripture as it relates to your specific circumstances.

For example, if your father deserted your family you can retrain your thoughts about God's faithfulness by meditating on Psalm 27:10, "Though my father and mother forsake me, the Lord will receive me." Or you can think about God's comforting promise in Hebrews 13:5 (NKJV*), "I will never leave you nor forsake you." God will *never* fail you, though that truth may be hard for you to believe. Regardless of what your feelings tell you in moments of despair, the truth is unchanging—God is always with you, loves you perfectly, and is a constant help in times of trouble.

Bill Hybels, in *Honest to God*, talks about the re-parenting that God can do in our lives:

> To a generation of men failed by their fathers and lost in a cloud of confusion, God says, "Don't spend a lifetime in aimless drifting. Don't succumb to mindless misinterpretations of masculine identity. Enter into a relationship with Me, through Jesus Christ, and allow *Me* to lead you into authentic manhood. Become my adopted sons and let me 're-father' you."
>
> To say that God wants to re-father His sons is no empty cliché. Scripture repeatedly presents God's desire to be personally and intimately involved with His children. He wants to provide the warmth, affection, discipline, and accountability that characterize a parent's loving relationship.
>
> But divine re-fathering is not a simple, overnight process. It's long-term, just like earthly fathering. It requires a commitment to two-way dialogue, through prayer and Bible study. It demands that

* *New King James Version.*

sons take time to listen to the Father's guidance, and then act on it. Sometimes men will have to seek the wisdom of others who know the Father better than they do. . . .

Adopted sons gradually will develop a more accurate sense of who they should be. Through His word and His personal direction, the perfect heavenly Father models and teaches authentic masculinity.[3]

ACCEPT AND BUILD ON WHAT YOU HAVE

The search to find something or someone here on earth to perfectly fill the father void in your life is a hopeless pursuit. No one is going to baby you through life and give you the attention and affection a four year old deserves and craves. You will add sorrow upon sorrow chasing down leads to some imaginary father-hero who will always be there for you. Don't waste your life looking for something you'll never be able to have, not because God doesn't want you to have it but because we live in a fallen world. Accept the imperfect fathering you received and invest your energy and time into understanding the perfect fathering you receive from your Father in heaven.

Direct your energy toward building healthy support relationships with friends and family members. Some well-meaning Christians will tell you just to forgive and forget past wrongs and move on in life. They imply that spiritual exercises such as reading the Bible or praying will solve your emotional problems, as if reading about being loved is the same as feeling loved. But prayer and Bible reading alone are not enough to bring about lasting change in your life—and God never said that they would be enough. We were created to need one another. God often shows His love for you through others, and He can provide the father-type love you need through others He chooses to bring into your life.

The Western model of education is derived from the Greek pattern. The ancient Greeks saw education as something that took place in a classroom where one knowledgeable person lectured to pupils, passing on what he knew. The Hebrew model of education was different. One person taught another by coming alongside and living out the truth to be learned in a life-application setting. That is the pattern Jesus set and the help you need. If your own father did not show you how to love and be loved, or how to parent your own children, pray that God will bring people into your life who can be role models and God's living truth in your life, manifesting God's love and concern for you in the flesh.

Russell remembered being beaten by his violent father, but he also remembered Bible stories he learned from an elderly neighbor. One Bible story, the story of the prodigal son, provided the strength Russell needed to survive and restore his sanity. "When Dad would hit me again and again, I would start to wonder what was wrong with me and why I couldn't love and get along with my dad. Then I would think of the father in the Bible who was always ready to love his son with open arms and never met his son with fists, no matter what. I told myself that fathers didn't always act the way mine did, and I went to church just to look around and prove to myself that I wasn't crazy. I met a friend my age and his family sort of adopted me—that has made all the difference in my life."

Even with God's help and supportive relationships with friends or family members, the chief responsibility for filling the father void in your life lies with you. Resist the urge to wait for your father, your friends, your spouse, or God to set your life straight. Take the initiative to change your thinking and lifestyle in ways that lead to a more fulfilling life. Part of maturity is taking responsibility for yourself and your emotional, spiritual, and physical needs.

Notes

1. Norman Wright, *Always Daddy's Girl: Understanding Your Father's Impact on Who You Are*, ed. Ed Stewart (Ventura, Calif.: Regal, 1989), p. 193.
2. Robert Hemfelt, Frank Minirth, and Paul Meier, *We Are Driven* (Nashville: Thomas Nelson, 1991), pp. 190-91.
3. Bill Hybels, *Honest to God* (Grand Rapids: Zondervan, 1990), pp. 35-36.

7

Seeing Life Through Father's Eyes

Julie, a thin woman with sandy brown hair, came to talk to me about persistent fatigue and feelings of depression. Lost in her personal world of pain, she stepped into my office in a daze and slid into a chair in the corner. When Julie noticed me get up from my desk to greet her, she stood to shake my hand with an obvious effort of forced friendliness. She looked, moved, and acted exhausted. Just being in her presence made me feel tired, and I suppressed the sudden urge to yawn.

After introductions and small talk, I asked Julie what brought her to see me. "I wish I knew," she responded. "I guess it's these feelings of being down almost all the time that are getting to me, and it's hard to find the energy to get through the day. I'm also pulling away more and more from other people—and that scares me."

To make sure there were no medical problems causing or complicating Julie's fatigue and depression, I asked about her basic health and medical history. Julie was not in the early stages of pregnancy, nursing a newborn, or going through hormonal changes. She had recently had a complete physical, her doctor reported that she was not anemic, her blood sugar levels were normal, and blood tests ruled out Chronic Fatigue Syndrome. She did not have mononucleosis, and none of the allergy medications she occasionally used had a history of producing side-effects similar to the symptoms that troubled her. In short, Julie's physician could not explain her chronic fatigue and depression.

Depression is usually the sign of deeper emotional conflicts. Therefore, I wanted to know what was going on in Julie's mind as well as in her life—and I knew father memories would bring that out. Julie gave a brief account of the activities she was involved in and how she felt about her roles. Then I asked her to share a couple of early father memories. The question hit a sensitive nerve. She looked away and her body stiffened. "Don't get me wrong, I love my father . . . it's just hard to think about my memories, that's all," she began.

"Do the best you can," I encouraged.

"Most of the memories I have of my father involve him being there but not being there, if you know what I mean," Julie said.

"Give me a couple of examples," I suggested, wanting her to be more specific.

"My father would bark out the orders, and the family was expected to fall in line and do what they were told," Julie recalled. "Everything he touched seemed to turn to gold except for me. No matter how hard I tried, I never seemed to measure up to the expectations he held for me. I tried—believe me, I tried—and I'm still trying. I know he still expects a lot. My sister has always been the golden girl—but not me.

"For example, back in '67 when I was ten years old, my dad started another restaurant in his chain. He already had several in operation. One Saturday he wanted me to go with him and help out busing tables. I remember how much I wanted to please him, and I guess I must have tried too hard. In the process I ended up dropping an entire tray of plates that smashed all over the floor. Dad just glared at me."

Julie went on to say that this was typical. No matter how hard she tried, she always felt as though she came in second in her father's eyes—second to her sister and second to his business. Things had not improved with time, and she still did not know clearly what was expected of her. And as it turned out, a lack of internal direction and feelings of never measuring up were the genesis of her depression. Her father memory was the key.

Julie's face showed visible emotion when she talked about her present relationship with her father. Her hands and voice trembled as she spoke. "I tried working for Dad, and that was a mistake. My sister manages one of the larger restaurants, and it runs like a dream. I quit. That was also a disaster. And when I tried to talk to him about some of my own plans for the future it turned into another argument. Now I'm tired of trying to please him."

"You said that everything your dad touched turned to gold—except for you?" I asked. "That's a pretty drastic statement."

"Well, that's the way it seems," Julie replied with a shrug.

"It seems to me that the all-or-nothing view you describe, setting up extreme polarities of golden-or-worthless, dream-or-disaster, never-or-always pleasing, and other such generalizations are distorting the way you see life," I said. "Except in dramatic movies, would you agree that most things in life fall somewhere in between *horrible* and *wonderful?*"

Julie grinned. "It does sound a little exaggerated when you say it."

Most of us will find that our memories are somewhat exaggerated —both the good and the bad events can take on a "bigger than life" aura. That is not necessarily because we intentionally stretch the story. Instead, we remember things through a child's eyes. That can make receiving a two-dollar truck for Christmas one of the most wonderful things that ever happened, or it can result in the desolation Julie was experiencing.

Little children personalize events to a great degree because a child's world revolves around himself and his immediate needs. Julie did that when she looked at the strain in her relationship with her father and concluded that she was the one who was deficient.

"Have you ever considered that your father blew it—not you? What if he wasn't Mr. Wonderful? He was too busy, too aloof, and too authoritarian for his family's good." I continued, "You see him as a success and bigger than life, and perhaps that's in part because others see him in that way and idolize his financial success. But the fact is, he missed out on being with you as he chased another dream. Like most of us, Julie, you made decisions early on in your life about your value, competence, and place. Unfortunately, you made some mistakes because you didn't see things in proper perspective. The truth is that you are a valuable, likable, capable woman."

Back in the 1950s and 1960s many of us were making our father memories. That was during a time when fathers, by and large, were into making money, not memories. When we put things in a cultural perspective, we find many loving but absent fathers. Men were busy being a success in a financial boom time. During those years it was virtually unheard of for fathers to stay at home with their children or to change their career goals in order to accommodate their families' needs.

Fathers in the '90s are generally more involved in family responsibilities, but they also have the nagging feeling that they must always be working harder at career success. As career and family compete for their time, mothers and fathers in the '90s are prone to making the same mistakes of their parents' generation by becoming loving—but absent—parents. Some individuals scrimp on the loving because they are so preoccupied with material gain that they fail to see the importance of nurturing their families. In Julie's case, in was clear that her father cared more about his business than his daughter.

In *The Blessing* Gary Smalley and John Trent write, "All of us long to be accepted by others. While we may say out loud, 'I don't care what other people think about me,' on the inside we all yearn for intimacy and affection. This yearning is especially true in our relationship with our parents. Gaining or missing out on parental approval has a tremendous effect on us, even if it has been years since we have had any regular contact with them."[1] That is exactly what Julie had spent a lifetime seeking—her father's approval. And all the time he had withheld it, remaining oblivious to her needs. The affect on Julie is great, but the possibility of his changing was slight. She needed to accept the reality of her father's deficiencies and change her thinking.

CLOSING THE SUPERMAN STORYBOOK

Even as an adult, Julie saw her father as a success and herself as a klutz. That was because a father figure takes on almost God-like stature in the eyes of a child. Most of us grew up with a "Father knows best" and "Dad is always right" outlook. But sooner or later we need to temper the Daddy-can do-no-wrong mind-set with a more mature understanding. We need to realize that fathers are people too, not supermen. They have feet of clay, not gold.

For individuals whose fathers adopted an arrogant, never-challenge-or-question-me stance, the road to adulthood often detours through the rocky field of rebellion or the valley of low self-esteem. When the child's approach to his father is reinforced by his abuse, violence often follows the in life of the child. Hitler's life is a good example of that process.

The harm Adolf Hitler brought upon the world had its roots in his father memories. Hitler wrote of repeatedly being whipped by his father and of the day he decided to shut off his tears, bottle up his anger, and turn it inward. He nourished that anger until it spewed onto the innocent victims of the Holocaust. Here is the father memory of a killer:

> I then resolved [after repeated physical abuse] never again to cry when my father whipped me. A few days later I had the opportunity of putting my will to the test. My mother, frightened, took refuge in front of the door. As for me, I counted silently the blows of the stick which lashed my rear end.[2]

Hitler's response to life was extreme, but the cycle of abuse is all too common. Yet it is not just cruel father memories that bring tears to my eyes. One day as I was listening to the radio I heard James Dobson share a moving story about a father whose little boy had leukemia. The effects of chemotherapy had caused all of the child's hair to fall out. The father was so overwhelmed with love for his little boy that when his son lost all of his hair, the father shaved his head also—leaving only the outline of the child's initials at the neckline.

That daddy didn't want his little boy to face the suffering alone. Compassion compelled him to identify himself with his son's baldness, easing his little boy's embarrassment and humiliation over being different. Despite the devastating effects of the cancer, that little boy will have an eternity to reflect on beautiful father memories. In a very healthy way, that child can say, "Daddy, you're my hero."

The gradual transition from Dad as the absolute authority in childhood to Dad as a respected and loved friend in adulthood goes most smoothly for those who are fortunate enough to be raised by a warm, humble man. A father who is quick to point the child to the perfection of his heavenly Father, and equally quick to admit and apologize for his own mistakes, will help his child close the superman storybook. The child will be able to internalize the healthy message that Daddy's not perfect—and that's OK, and

I'm not perfect—and that's OK too. God and Daddy love me just the way I am.

It is natural and good for a child to have a sense of respect for his father and to look up to him. But Julie had set her father on a pedestal. She needed to dethrone Dad so that she could relate to him eye-to-eye, adult-to-adult. Making an effort to see life through her father's eyes would help Julie, and others like her, to see the reality of her father's humanity.

Julie gained a more realistic measure of her father by taking the steps listed below. I will explain each one in detail in the remainder of the chapter.

> She brought Dad down to normal stature—no pedestals, please
> She became an observer versus a reactor
> She looked at her father's childhood relationship with his dad
> She looked at the family "road map" (more about the "road map" later)
> She started immediately. Do it now, it impacts your life today

No Pedestals, Please

During a recent trip to Washington, D.C., my son Evan and I toured the Capitol building. After clearing security we climbed the stairs to the balcony overlooking the House chambers. After a time of reflection and appreciation for our country, we began the long walk through the corridors that led to the Senate chambers. Along the way we came to a stately room that houses the statues of many of America's founding fathers.

As I looked up into the bronzed, frozen faces of these bigger-than-life men whose presence loomed over us, I was reminded again of how easy it is to make our fathers and our father memories bigger than they really are.

After Evan and I left the Capitol, we walked the two miles down the mall, past the Washington monument, past the Vietnam memorial, and up the granite stairs that lead to the imposing sculpture of Abraham Lincoln. President Lincoln, as you know, sits confidently in a position of authority. When you pause for reflection at Lincoln's feet, you feel a sense of awe, as if you are treading on sacred ground.

I told Julie about my trip to Washington and then said to her, "You are looking at your father that way, Julie. As I hear you talk about him, he seems more like one of these lifeless, powerful, granite statues than a father of flesh-and-blood. You have etched his put-downs in the stone around his pedestal as a constant reminder of your imagined inadequacies and have shrunk your own personhood, gifts, and talents by comparison."

A healthy daddy/daughter or father/son relationship at any age is not based upon superiority/inferiority comparisons. Dad is not God. It is not he who should pronounce you good. Your father was and is just a man, not the Supreme Being. His wisdom may be worth careful attention, but he was and is imperfect and capable of misjudgment and mistakes. As adults we come to respect and honor our fathers as equals—neither inferior in importance nor superior in value to ourselves.

We may live in our father's shadow because we saw him as a definer of reality when we were children. He was the provider, trainer, leader, and authority figure who shaped many of the values and perceptions we carry to this day. Our reputations may be linked to his. We may even inherit a generic disposition toward a similar temperament, similar medical problems, and a similar body build. But we are more than just a "chip off the old block"— we are a complete and whole block in and of ourselves. We need to understand that our true identity is separate from our father and should not be confused, mixed up, or merged with the image of the family name.

The dual relationship of father and equal is brought out in the Bible. When the adult child and his parents are joined as part of the family of God through faith in Christ, he and his parents stand in a different relation to one another than before. Now Dad and Mom are not only the adult child's parents but his brother and sister in Christ. It is the equal-standing-before-God relationship that characterizes healthy adult-to-adult love. That relationship is not one of disrespect, but rather is one of supreme mutual respect and unconditional acceptance. As a child develops his own identity as an adult, he needs to respect the differences that hold between himself and his father, not look down on his father for being different from himself.

As Julie and I continued our counseling sessions, I encouraged her to begin the process of dethroning her father. To help her look at life through her father's eyes I gave her an exercise for learning to become an observer and responder, not just a reactor, in her relationship to her father.

LEARNING TO BE AN OBSERVER-RESPONDER

When our three babies were born they came out demanding their own sweet way. They quickly learned that crying brought food, a dry bottom, and lots of attention from Mom and Dad. They were learning to react to their world and to act in ways that brought forth an immediate response to their needs. All of us went through a similar process of reacting to our environment and attempting to set things up to suit ourselves.

Many of the life-directing beliefs we carry are the result of our accommodating those self-centered attitudes. If you grew up in an abusive family you likely learned to react to violence by hiding from it or by giving in to the perpetrator. If you were raised in an encouraging home you probably learned to react to others with smiles and warmth, expecting them to return in kind. We all learned early how to best maneuver ourselves and manipulate others to meet our needs.

Unfortunately, not all of the knee-jerk reactions useful to us as children are effective and appropriate for adults. A tantrum might be "cute" (or at least bearable) in curly-haired, eighteen-month-old Patty, but if tantrums become grown-up Patricia's habitual response to stress she will be a difficult woman to live with. Mikey might be able to bully his little brother to get his way, but it will not be the most effective way for adult Michael to win friends and influence people!

As an adult becomes aware of the patterns of behavior he has established in his relationship with his father, he can start to break the cycle that led to those inappropriate ways of responding. Then he can replace those defective reactions with effective responses that lead to more loving relationships with Dad and others.

Take a step or two away from your father and try to answer the following questions from an emotional distance. Be objective, and fill in the blanks as if you were an impartial observer. This "father-watching" quiz will help you determine if you are a reactor or observer. Try it by yourself first. If you have difficulty, enlist the help of other friends or family members later.

1. What was your father's greatest fear in life? _____
_____

2. How would you characterize your father's communication with his father? _____
_____

3. Did you ever see your father cry? _____ Over what?
_____
If not, why? _____

4. What made your father laugh? _____

5. How did your father respond to criticism? _____
Why? _____

6. What kind of grades did your father get during school?
_____

7. What are or were some dreams your father had that he never accomplished? _____
What dreams did he achieve? _____
_____

8. As a child, how did your father relate to his father?
_____
To his siblings? _____

9. What was the history of his courtship with your mother?
_____
_____

10. List in order of importance, your father's five top priorities in life. _____
_____

Reactors will have trouble answering those questions. If the answers didn't come to mind, perhaps you do not really know your father as well as you thought you did but simply react to him.

A lifetime of reacting rather than interacting doesn't prepare you well to be an observer. Reactors don't probe or initiate. They see themselves as objects rather than subjects. Interactors respond rather than move like puppets when their emotional strings are pulled.

As Julie labored to answer the questions she realized that she knew very little about her father or his outlook on life. "I guess I really don't understand what makes Dad the man he is or why he acts the way he does," Julie admitted.

"Julie, that's my point," I said. "Until you start to understand what makes your father tick you will never get a handle on your reaction to him." As Julie looked out the window toward the mountains, I pointed out that she had become proficient at reacting to her father's critical look, silence, and aloofness. But she needed to see what brought on those behaviors and how she could use nondefensive communication to establish new habits of response.

LOOKING AT YOUR FATHER'S FATHER MEMORIES

Many beliefs, values, goals, and behavior are passed down through the generations. Sayings like "He's a chip off the old block," or "Like father like son," or "It runs in the family" are common because they reflect what often happens. Most children are in some way "cut from the same bolt of cloth" as their parents and grandparents.

That means that exploring your father's childhood memories can be a fascinating way to learn more about him and gain insight about yourself as well. During the writing of *Unlocking the Secrets of Your Childhood Memories* I spent weeks collecting the early memories of famous people, friends, clients, and family members. But for me personally, the most meaningful memories were those of my own parents. They hit home and brought my mom and dad into clear focus.

Admittedly, the thought of your father's running around in diapers, taking his first steps, going off to school for the first time, or going on a date can bring a blank stare. But if you really want to get to know your father better and see life from his eyes—and you are fortunate enough to have Dad around to talk to—do it! It can be an enriching experience for both of you.

As my parents shared their own memories from childhood I was reminded that parents have problems, too. They struggle with the same kind of personal concerns, issues, insecurities, and fears we do; they experience the same gamut of emotions, pain, expectations, disappointments, and delight we do.

My father is the king of projects. He never met an idea he didn't like to think about. He has more projects rattling around in his head than could be done in three lifetimes. He is goal-oriented and has the stick-to-itiveness of flypaper. When he gets going, watch out!

I have always respected my dad for his ability to turn an idea into a reality benefiting worthwhile humanitarian and Christian causes. He has accepted many ambitious projects to help others. So it was no surprise that my father's earliest memory was of building a scooter out of two pieces of wood and a couple of skates. As he told the memory his face lit up with delight. Every detail was in place, and before long he had finished the project all by himself. I chuckled as my dad shared the memory because it was just typical "Dad"—which means to dream it, plan it, do it!

It was fun to imagine my father as a little boy who was pleased with himself for completing a project. As we exchanged more memories I gained a new appreciation for my parents. During that special evening my wife gave me a few nudges, as if to say, "So *that* explains it! Now I know where you came by that habit." By planning a similar evening of conversation with your own family, you can learn more about your parents and help your spouse understand your background.

LOOKING AT THE FAMILY ROAD MAP

The process of looking backward at your psychological and cultural heritage is part of discovering what I call the family "road map." As I explained to Julie, a "family road map is what counselors call a genogram, but it's actually nothing more than an emotional, spiritual, and relational family tree. The diagrams help us see how we reached where we are today, both individually and as a family."

A FAMILY ROAD MAP

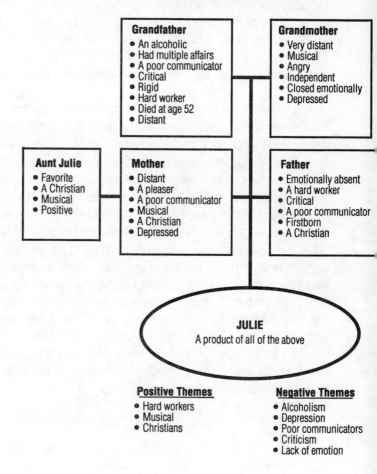

Grandfather
- An alcoholic
- Had multiple affairs
- A poor communicator
- Critical
- Rigid
- Hard worker
- Died at age 52
- Distant

Grandmother
- Very distant
- Musical
- Angry
- Independent
- Closed emotionally
- Depressed

Aunt Julie
- Favorite
- A Christian
- Musical
- Positive

Mother
- Distant
- A pleaser
- A poor communicator
- Musical
- A Christian
- Depressed

Father
- Emotionally absent
- A hard worker
- Critical
- A poor communicator
- Firstborn
- A Christian

JULIE
A product of all of the above

Positive Themes
- Hard workers
- Musical
- Christians

Negative Themes
- Alcoholism
- Depression
- Poor communicators
- Criticism
- Lack of emotion

Uncle John
- An alcoholic
- Musical
- A hard worker
- A poor communicator
- Multiple marriages

Uncle Frank
- Dad's favorite
- A hard worker
- A poor communicator

Uncle Ken
- Irresponsible
- Uninvolved
- An alcoholic

We are genetically related to those who went on before us and often pick up their vision or values. As we see each ancestor's part in the jigsaw puzzle of behaviors, attitudes, and beliefs that have been passed down generationally, the picture we have of our father will round out and we can understand why he was the kind of father he was and is—and, significantly, the kind of father he was never destined to be. Not only are the sins and shortcomings of one generation often passed along to the next, as the Bible mentions, but family strengths and positive characteristics are transmitted, too. We receive a mixed bag of gifts and griefs from our lineage, including our inborn talents and temperament as well as our early training.

As you draw your father's family tree, refer to the example from Julie's family on pages 108-9 for help. When you get to your father's level of the family tree, talk with him about the points outlined in the section of the list below devoted to him. Issues to get down in print include the following:

Your father's grandparents
Nationalities
Relationships
Occupations
Religion
Positive characteristics
Negative characteristics

Your father's parents
How affection was demonstrated
Who was in control
Who had the power and in what area
Income
Priorities
Education
Divorces and remarriages
Community and church involvement

Your father and his siblings
Who got the best deal
Who got the worst deal
Relationships—close, pleasant, hostile
Birth order
Stepbrother(s) or -sister(s)

Your father
>   His earliest memories
>   What he enjoys most
>   What he likes and dislikes most about his life thus far
>   What he likes most about himself
>   His attitude toward marriage, including male and female
>   roles
>   His attitude toward church and beliefs about God

Julie worked on the project in the week that followed. She listed both positive and negative dominant themes. When she returned for her next appointment, she had a clearer picture of her father and a new understanding of what made him tick. That was because she had discovered several attitudes and tendencies in his behavior that helped her recognize underlying issues that were a factor in the tension in their relationship.

For example, while doing her family tree, Julie discovered that her father was a firstborn of four boys and showed an interest in detail, control, responsibility, and perfection typical of oldest sons. Her father's brothers had succeeded in their own areas, but her father was singled out to follow in the family business and someday take over. When her father was only twenty-three his father died and the business was indeed passed on to him. His mother was uninvolved in the restaurant operation and quickly remarried. Julie's father was left with overwhelming responsibilities.

Julie's grandfather was an alcoholic, which led in part to his early death. Julie discovered that communication had always been a weak point in him. So at least two generations of her family had been off-course, pursuing wrong priorities with little regard for one another. Julie's study showed that her father was the product of years of sin and selfishness.

Julie's father and Julie herself were the recipients of a heritage of neglect, perfectionism, rigidity, repression, poor communication, and a lack of affection and fun. It was a breakthrough for July to write out the road map of the path her family had taken and was now headed down. Julie said firmly, "I can see desperation, rejection, loneliness, and emptiness written all over the lives on this page. And I will *not live* my life this way. Starting with me, our family is going to head in a new direction!"

For the first time in her life Julie could see her father for what he was—the product of sin and continuing in a pattern of sin by choice—a real person entangled in a web of dysfunctional and unloving relationships. When Julie saw how high the stakes were, she refused to participate in the twisted games her family played. She would not accept her father's declaration that she was unworthy and unable to amount to anything—he was wrong, and the whole family was in the wrong.

Most individuals who sincerely work at laying out a family tree and road map discover things they want to change. But they also discover encouraging characteristics and direction and patterns in their family that they appreciate and want to imitate. They are generally pleased to see that doing good "comes naturally" or "just feels right" in those areas. For example, the man who comes from a family with a strong work ethic has been trained and shown how to plan, initiate, and complete the work at hand. He can make the most of this healthy heritage by applying his willingness and ability to work for the good of his own family, church, and community. And he can keep his time at work balanced by time for play, rest, and family togetherness.

The goal is not to denounce your past or disown your family. It is to come to see your family's strengths and weaknesses as they really are. Then you can work at celebrating and making the most of your healthy heritage while at the same time minimizing the effect of the less desirable characteristics. Don't let yourself be pulled into self-destructive patterns or sinful styles of relating that have been established by past generations.

History doesn't have to repeat itself. Let God and His Word direct your life, not the words and expectations handed down through the generations of your family. If the process of doing that is too overpowering or confusing, seek the help of a counselor, pastor, or trusted friend.

Hearing and understanding undiscovered truth about your father and your patterns of relating to him, like Julie did, will only get you to second base. To hit a home run you not only need to hear and understand but must also believe the truth and act on it. Julie needed not only to realize the lies she was living by but to look beyond her father memories and see her father as the man he was in the present.

Do It Now

Up to this point in counseling, Julie's eyes had been blinded. When she saw her father she saw only a powerful, intimidating, and successful person. She saw a person of authority, not a flesh-and-blood father, and certainly not a friend. In fact, the likelihood of a friendship developing between Julie and her father seemed as great as the possibility of lightening hitting twice in the same spot.

I explained to Julie that friendship with her father and growth in their present relationship didn't necessarily mean being pals and buddies or going fishing every weekend. Friendship meant changing their roles from a "parent-to-inept-child" relationship to an "adult-to-capable-adult" relationship.

In the weeks that followed, Julie began to see herself as a valuable person worthy of respect. Her actions, body language, eye contact, and energy level changed. Without words, she communicated to her father the thought *I believe in myself,* and a remarkable change occurred. As Julie demonstrated self-respect and healthy self-esteem, her father began to show more confidence in her abilities and came to respect and esteem her more.

It may be impossible for you to become best friends with your father, but I encourage you—as much as it depends upon you, without pressuring him—to make the effort to improve the quality of your relationship. Time is short. Before you know it your father will be gone—and the opportunity for friendship will be over.

Recently, I ran across a song by Mark Gersmehl that beautifully expresses the changing roles of parent and child. It is called "Love Them While We Can":

> They tied our shoes, took us to school
> Patched our worn-out jeans
> They soothed our tears and childish fears
> And listened to our dreams
> Somewhere along the golden years
> Their hair has lost its sheen
> The notes to hymn 110 crackle when they sing
>
> Now they are alone,
> No children's voices
> Filling up their home.

We must love, love them while we can
We must love, love them while we can

The folks that taught us our first words
Still have much to say
The silver secrets of this world
Lie beneath those crowns of gray.
As they approach the end,
We change our role
From children to best friend

We must love, love them while we can
We must love, love them while we can

We always thought they'd be around
'Til the end of time
'Til one day we wake and find . . .

We must love, love them while we can
We must love, love them while we can[3]

As I am writing this chapter my seventy-five-year-old father is critically ill in a local hospital. After seven years and eighteen major surgeries, his future health is at best questionable. Over this time we have been forced into changing roles. I have always seen my father as the strong protector of the family. Filled with strength, he has been the one to set the goals and get things done. But now the roles have changed. No longer can he do what he once could. Yet inside he is still the man I remember, though his body can no longer cooperate. And the changing roles have reinforced the truth of Mark Gersmehl's lyrics.

NOTES

1. Gary Smalley and John Trent, *The Blessing* (Nashville: Thomas Nelson, 1986), p. 9.
2. John Toland, *Adolf Hitler* (New York: Doubleday, 1976), pp. 12-13.
3. Written by Mark Gersmehl. Copyright © 1983 Bug and Bear Music. Exclusive adm. by LCS Music Group, Inc., P.O. Box 815129, Dallas, TX 75381. Int'l Copyright Securied. All Rights Reserved. Used By Permission.

8

If Dad Should Die
Before I Wake

When Dave was in junior high his father died. He was very close to his dad, sharing similar interests and spending a great deal of time with him, so the loss left him overwhelmingly sad and lonely. By temperament Dave was quite different from, and had never felt close to, his mother. During the difficult years that followed his father's death, they quarreled over just about everything. Then, when Dave was a sophomore in college, it came to a head.

Dave explained, "At the beginning of the second semester I changed my major. It was the second switch, and my mom, who feels threatened by change, blew up at me. When she started to use the same old guilt tactics I confronted her. I guess I'd had some time to figure things out at college and wasn't willing to put up with being treated that way any longer."

Guilt from the Grave

Whenever Dave's mother felt frustrated by her inability to relate to and control Dave's behavior she resorted to pushing the guilt button with comments such as, "What would your father think of that?" or, "How do you think your dad would feel if he saw how you're acting?" or, "I just want to help you make good decisions [sniff, sniff] so that Dad would be proud of you." Dave's mother borrowed authority from the strength of the father-son bond and used her son's vulnerable spot to manipulate him.

CONSIDER THE SOURCE

Dave was determined to choose his own vocation, though, and he was beginning to recognize his mother's insecurity and destructive use of the past for leverage in present disagreements. Dave's father memories validated his misgivings about his mother's remarks, and he began to consider the source. He decided to confront his mother calmly the next time the behavior occurred, and he mentally rehearsed what he would say.

So when she challenged his decision to switch majors with a comment about what his dad would think, Dave responded frankly, "The Dad *I* remember—the Dad I knew and loved—successfully switched professions, not just majors, at least four times. Dad always encouraged me to try new things and to find and develop my strengths. If he were alive today, Dad would not be bothered by my decision. I resent having you impose imaginary conflict between Dad and me to get your way. That's just not the way it was or is. Dad was proud of me and still would be. Mom, your memory serves you well, but it's all a lie!"

An emotional exchange followed and many past hurts were brought into the open. Although Dave and his mother suffered a temporary rift in their relationship following the conflict, over time it worked out for the better. They set up new, healthier ground rules for relating to one another.

First and foremost, Dave stated his position regarding conversations about his dad. He insisted that he would not allow speculation about what his father would think in regard to any present actions. His mother could openly express any of her feelings, but she could not pass them off as his father's viewpoint.

ACTIONS SPEAK LOUDER THAN INTENTIONS

Dave and his mother had good intentions about trying to improve communication between them, but without clearly defined limits and consequences it was unlikely that lasting change would occur. Bad habits die hard.

Dave wisely used more than words to state his position—he backed them up with ground rules for action. There were no surprises. Dave made clear to his mother ahead of time that whenever she slipped into past manipulative habits he would bring it to her attention. If her approach was not changed immediately, Dave would end the conversation or the visit. No arguments. No emotional scenes. They would interact according to the healthy boundaries they had established, or not at all.

I realize that kind of accountability may seem harsh, but Dave had to be firm. He treasured his memories of his father's love and could not let anyone—even his mother—attempt to destroy what he cherished so deeply. Because Dave's father could not set matters straight, Dave had to speak the truth in love.

Dave is establishing a healthy boundary, walling his mother out of the past relational bond between him and his dad. The boundary he has drawn requires that his mother treat him as a decision-making adult, not as a little boy or as an extension of her own life. By contrast, codependents yield interpersonal boundaries and merge with others. Charles Sells, in *Unfinished Business,* says, "The co-dependent's problem is one of boundaries. To be separate from your parents, you must develop your own identity apart from them."[1]

Sometimes a parent clings to an overprotective role and tries to exert too much control over the adult child. At other times, as parents age or face serious illness, their adult children become overprotective caretakers. Both parent and child can cross healthy borders. Even parents who have passed away can exert an unhealthy influence when their children yield to imagined parental control or live out the parent's prophecy of what their life would become. Here are ten questions to ask yourself to determine if a lack of boundaries with a parent(s) is a problem for you:[2]

1. Do you think you know what is best for your parents?
2. Do you need your parents' approval?
3. When your parents hurt you, do you seem to feel it more than they do?
4. If members of your family have had a bad day, do you react?
5. Do you feel you must solve your parents' problems (or believe they have to help you solve your problems)?
6. Do you respond more to your family's interests than develop your own?

7. Do you limit your involvement with others because of your parents?
8. Do you think you can convince members of your family to like themselves?
9. Do you consider carefully what you say to your parents in order to get the right reaction from them?
10. Do you feel guilty for taking care of yourself (or for not taking care of them)?

Is there someone in your life who drags up the past, or distorts the past, in your present relationships? Whenever someone uses false guilt, or even true guilt, to hurt or control you, a warning beeper should go off. Guilt motivation is a clue that something unhealthy is happening. Like Dave, you may need to set limits on certain relationships and back them up with clear consequences. Learn to practice constructive and calm confrontation. But don't establish guidelines for behavior and interpersonal boundaries if you are unwilling to patrol the border. Actions speak louder than intentions.

Beth's father isn't dead, but he might as well be. Nine years ago he split the scene, leaving Beth and her mother floundering. In some ways it would have been a cleaner wound if he had died. The balance of the family system was destroyed, and Beth's mom could never restore the family's equilibrium. In trying to fill the emotional void, she turned her attention to being the "best mom" she could be. However, the best of intentions don't always make the best of sense. Beth's mom hovered over her like a mother hen.

Beth's mother pulled in the reins and exerted too much control over her well-developed sixteen-year-old daughter. Afraid that she would lose her daughter as she had her husband, Beth's mother held on too tight, too long. At a time when Beth should have been spreading her wings, Mom was clipping them.

Even when Beth left home to get married, she felt pressure to be Mother's little girl. Phone calls, visits, and notes received over the years reinforced the message. When Beth confronted her mother over the issue, her mother denied that there was a problem. Yet counseling experience confirms that it is not unusual for a parent to become overinvested in his children following the death or departure of the other parent, as Beth's mother did.

Beth, like Dave, needed to set boundaries with her mother. Every situation is different, but here is a summary of an approach to setting boundaries.

Remember your goal:	"Mom, it's time for me to grow up and be on my own. I can't be everything you want me to be. I love you and want us to develop a good friendship, but I need to make my own decisions."
Remember that parents have feelings too:	"Mom, I don't want to hurt your feelings, but we need to resolve a couple of issues between us. Specifically, I feel like you expect me to spend most of my free time with you. And that's not practical."
Start out small:	"I can't meet all your emotional needs, Mom. I love you, and I want to be here for you, but I need space for myself and my family. I need to limit how much time we spend together—this is best for both of us."
Be specific:	"If your schedule is open, how about spending Thursday nights together. We could go out to dinner and then spend the evening together."

As you begin this process, think ahead to anticipate disagreements that may arise. Mentally rehearse how you will respond to each verbal attack with a nondefensive statement, such as:

- "I'm sorry you feel that way . . ."
- "When you _____ I feel _____ because _____."
- "I understand what you're saying, but I don't agree."

Because emotional games or harsh or negative criticism often get the job done when people want to control others, parents and children may slip into destructive communication styles. Don't allow your discussion to degenerate to that level. Refuse to raise your voice, play on people's emotions, or listen to lies. Control the conversation and control yourself to avoid creating more problems than you solve.

AVOID TRIANGLES—TWO'S COMPANY, THREE'S UNHEALTHY!

Another rule of thumb for healthy communication within the family, church, work environment, or community is to avoid triangles. Avoid talking to Dick through Jane—simply go directly to Dick yourself and talk. Don't complain to a church board member about last week's sermon. See the pastor himself and talk things through in private. Don't whine to Mom that Dad is being unfair— choose the proper time and calmly voice your feelings to Dad in person.

But what happens when you can't speak in person? The need to avoid triangles is especially important where it concerns a deceased individual, whether the one who passed away was a family member, the founder of the company, or an influential friend. It is not uncommon for individuals to lend power to their opinions by making reference to the (supposed) wishes of a departed loved one. Dave was right to insist that his mother not speak for his deceased father.

If your father is no longer living, or is no longer able to communicate his thoughts clearly, beware of accepting the negative pronouncements of a go-between regarding your father's view of what is being done. Your mother, stepmother, or sibling should not be interpreting your relationship with Dad. Widowed or divorced mothers who are reading this book should also take to heart the warning against using the father-child relationship for leverage in controlling your children's behavior.

RULING FROM THE GRAVE

No one had to remind Stephen of his father's expectations, before or after his father's death. Although Stephen looked like he had just walked off the television set for "Prime Time Live," he was a deeply troubled man. His perfectly tailored suit, distinguished appearance, and slightly graying hair added to the polished image of Mr. Perfectly Informed. Stephen had achieved notable success in the news broadcasting field, but he came to see me because of a nagging sense of emptiness.

Although Stephen's dad had been dead for many years, it was clear that his father still ran the show. When I asked Stephen about his early father memories, Stephen hung his head slightly and responded, "When I was about eight I brought my current affairs report from my *Weekly Reader* home from school and showed it to Dad. I thought he would be pleased, but instead he read it carefully, then told me I would never amount to much if I didn't do better work. He went on to critique what I wrote and explain where my thinking was shallow or my opinions based on inaccurate assumptions. I suppose he meant well, but I was crushed."

"How did that incident affect your relationship?" I asked, sensing that this childhood episode was the key to unlocking Stephen's present emotional distress.

"I decided I would do better next time. I would think harder and study the subject more—no one would ever catch me looking foolish again," Stephen said. "In one respect, I guess I owe my success to that decision."

"You have been very successful," I replied, "Do you enjoy what you do? Does it bring you a great deal of satisfaction to do your job so well?"

"No, not really, " Stephen said sadly. "The dad I carry inside of me still nags that I could have done better, that I said or wrote something stupid, that no matter how hard I aim to please it won't be enough."

Stephen's life was being guided from the grave by his father, or more accurately by Stephen's inner dialogue focused on his father perceptions. All of Stephen's efforts to succeed were directed at gaining his father's approval. While he was alive, Stephen's father had withheld his blessing and encouragement of Stephen as a person and of Stephen's work. Now that Stephen's father was dead, Stephen was left chasing an impossible dream. The father-son relationship would never be what Stephen had hoped. The blessing was out of reach. Gary Smalley and John Trent say of people like Stephen: "Such people can spend years struggling to free themselves from their past and as a result are never free to enjoy a commitment relationship in the present. If hurtful patterns from the past are not broken, they are likely to repeat themselves in the next generation."[3]

SELF-DEFINITION

Stephen was allowing himself to be defined by his dad's projected opinion from the past. He was still trying to prove himself after all those years. Regardless of how well people conduct themselves or how successful they appear, many individuals, like Stephen, don't feel good about themselves. Even though they are productive citizens they feel inadequate—like failures and rejects —much of the time. Because they believe they have failed to meet their father's and their own expectations they constantly struggle to measure up. They cannot replace a dead father's approval, so no achievement gives them the opportunity of reaching the goal.

Kevin Leman writes about breaking such a cycle in *Measuring Up:*

> The more years I spend as a psychologist, the more I am convinced of the truth of that old saying "As the twig is bent, so grows the tree."
>
> The things that happen to us very early in life will shape the way we live out the rest of our years. Even if they live to be 120, most people will be following the life-style that was built into them by the time they were four or five years old.[4]

All too often a father's negative pronouncements or disappointments become negative, self-fulfilling prophecy. Happily, the opposite is also true. Encouragement from Dad and statements of affirmation can have a lasting, positive impact on the child.

The notion had been drummed into Stephen's subconscious that a person's worth was determined by the quality of his work, and he was doing everything he could to prove to his dad and to himself that he was a person of value. I instructed him to meditate every morning and evening for a week on the following simple truth statements:

- I am not defined by my work. I am a valuable person with or without my profession.

- My desire to do well and my honest hard work are acceptable and pleasing to my heavenly Father, regardless of how I imagine my dad would have reacted.
- God is not disappointed in me when I do my best, and I do not need to be disappointed with myself. I am loved and accepted by God, and I can love and accept myself.
- Even the most intelligent and informed people still make mistakes. It's OK to be human; no one is perfect.
- By acting with integrity and diligence I have brought honor to our family name. I can give myself permission to feel good about my success.
- My best is good enough. I am capable of doing good work. I don't need to measure up to shifting standards of absolute perfection.
- There are others in my life who approve of me and can counteract this one source of negative feedback.

"FOLLOW YOUR FEELINGS" IS BAD ADVICE

If you were raised by critical parents the last thing you should do is to follow your feelings. Every time there's room for improvement your feelings will tell you that you are inadequate, that you'll never get things right. Your feelings will lie to you and make you think that things will never improve and that nothing you can do now will change your fate. Don't believe it!

Things can change.

Take time now to evaluate any father messages that are bouncing around in your head. List both positive and negative statements that come to mind. If your father is dead it is essential that you take the initiative to deal with each of those evaluations and redirect your thinking wherever necessary. You must find resolution within yourself because it is no longer possible to resolve the issues with your father.

Even if your father is still living, you hold the key to your own life. As an adult you must choose to accept or reject the validity of your father's evaluations and expectations according to God's truth, not according to your feelings. Like Stephen, you will need to set your self-talk straight. When you reason things through in your mind, look for the lies you repeat and correct them.

Instead of thinking about or scolding yourself with what your critical father would have said, imagine what he should have said or done as a loving, nurturing father. That can be a healing process as you realize that *you* as an adult can re-parent the inner child inside you and treat yourself with the respect and kindness you deserve as one of God's special creations.

DON'T SPEAK ILL OF THE DEAD?

If your father is no longer living, don't expect a great deal of help from others in the process of evaluating your relationship. There is a strong sentiment against speaking negatively of the dead. To some degree the tendency to gloss over the bad and focus on the good is healthy. But a common denominator in dysfunctional families is a joint conspiracy to cover up family problems, even to the degree of distorting history or reality.

One young pastor was called to do a funeral for Mr. Grosbart, a notable citizen who was known for carousing, sarcastic comments about the church, and blatant disinterest in his daughter's well-being. The pastor remarked with a sigh, "It would be so much easier if I could just drop the pretense of his being a fine, upstanding citizen, implying that he is now living happily in heaven. Simply put, Mr. Grosbart chose to live without God, and he died without God. How can I look at the hurt in his daughter's eyes and honor the dead man who neglected her?"

Just because your father may have come to a tragic end or died of a cruel disease doesn't mean that the rush of sympathy toward him should sweep the character of his life under the rug. If the eulogy doesn't match what you know of his life, don't take it at face value.

In the Bible we are told to honor our fathers and our mothers, and I would not want to be misunderstood as encouraging anyone to do otherwise. But facing the reality of flaws in your father relationship does not have to lead to slanderous statements, rebellion, disrespect, or other sinful responses. At the same time, neither will ignoring or refusing to talk about problems bring lasting change in those who must find healing for damaged emotions and past pain.

PUTTING RESPONSIBILITY WHERE IT BELONGS

If you had a destructive or abusive relationship with your dad, it is important for you to internalize this message:

> I am not responsible for the painful events in
> my childhood that stemmed from my father's
> sin. I let go of his responsibility.

Many of my clients have wrongly blamed themselves for things a little child has no control over. Learning to put the responsibility where it belongs is difficult for them. In *Toxic Parents* Susan Forward recommends the following exercise as a way of releasing yourself from things your parents did that were not your fault and cannot be changed. I pass the exercise along to you with the encouragement to pray about each of the issues as you complete the exercise.

To make effective use of the exercise, set aside a quiet, private time for talking to the child within you. To help you visualize how little and helpless you were as a child, you might want to use a childhood photograph. Say out loud to that child, "You were not responsible for . . ." and finish the sentence with every item on the list that applies to your life.

"You were not responsible for . . . ."

1. the way they neglected or ignored you
2. the way they made you feel unloved or unlovable
3. their cruel or thoughtless teasing
4. the bad names they called you
5. their unhappiness
6. their problems
7. their choice not to do anything about their problems
8. their drinking
9. what they did when they were drinking
10. their hitting you
11. their molesting you

Add any other painful, repetitive experiences that you have always felt responsible for. Then, to bring more sharply into focus who was really responsible for your mistreatment—your parent— go back through the list, repeating each item that applies to your childhood, but this time preceding the statements with the words, "My parents were responsible for . . ." Again, add anything that is relevant to your personal experience.[5]

Even though you may realize intellectually that what you experienced was not your fault, the child inside may still feel responsible. You may need to repeat the exercise several times and remind yourself not to assume misplaced guilt.

Although you were not responsible for your parents' actions in the past, you are responsible for the way you have responded over the years. Separate your disobedient behavior that was rightfully and appropriately punished from any unjust treatment you received. Then seek forgiveness from God for the wrongs you committed and the times you hurt your parents or sinned in your responses. Ask God to forgive you for any unloving actions or attitudes you have harbored. By claiming the biblical truth of 1 John 1:9 you can experience the emotional freedom of a perfectly clean slate, wiped free of guilt and the stain of hate.

Consider the power of this promise: "If we claim to be without sin, we deceive ourselves and the truth is not in us. If we confess our sins [to God], he is faithful and just and will forgive us our sins and purify us from all unrighteousness" (1 John 1:8-9). If you pray for forgiveness you may not feel forgiven, but you can accept the truth that you are forgiven because God promised you would be. It may take some time for your feelings to catch up with your new awareness that you have truly been set free from the guilt of the past.

CONFRONTATION WITH A DEAD PARENT

Many people find it helpful to have a constructive confrontation with their father to resolve or at least acknowledge childhood issues. But if one or both of your parents are dead there is no outlet for that release. Here are several ways to handle your need for a heart-to-heart talk.

One means of expression that can be effective is to write a letter to your father explaining the feelings, thoughts, or regrets you have been holding in. Then read the letter aloud at the grave-side, to a photograph of your father, or to an empty chair. Imagine your father's actual presence as you release your anxiety and hurt.

Some persons prefer to role-play with a trusted counselor, where the counselor stands in for the father. Of course, the sharing of such personal and emotionally charged responses to your childhood must only be done in strictest confidence. Other persons are most at ease with pouring their hearts out to their heavenly Father and letting Him absorb the hurt and rejection from the past. That is a powerful form of healing provided through the grace and mercy of our perfect Father.

I once counseled a middle-aged woman struggling with negative feelings toward her deceased father. Talking, writing, and even prayer did not relieve the hurt. So I suggested that she do something that would get her physically involved in the process. I had her lay her memories to rest by literally burying them. And it worked.

She took her notes, filled with pain and hurt from her past, dug a hole, and actually buried them in the ground. Burying the notebook became for her a physical representation of the spiritual and emotional decision she had made—but didn't yet feel—to forgive her father. The tangible act symbolized her inner commitment and helped her emotions come into line with her will.

Talking through or writing out sensitive issues will not be easy. You may find it extremely uncomfortable. But if using a substitute parent helps you heal self-defeating mental and emotional wounds it is worth the pain. If your childhood was traumatic I encourage you to enlist the support of a pastor, counselor, or close friend as you confront issues from your childhood.

On the Bright Side

The imagination is a wonderful, God-given tool not only to help heal past hurts but also to make the most of good experiences. Those who were fortunate enough to have many good memories of their dad can imagine and move toward recreating those good times with their own children. Rita remembers singing with her father and now says, "When we sing together as a family I can feel Dad's pleasure. It would have pleased him so much to join in. I can almost see him smiling down at us."

Linda, a cheerful and compassionate woman, remarked following her father's death, "I know that Dad loved Jesus with all his heart and is living with Him now in heaven. On days when I desperately miss my dad, it helps to imagine him living in a land of no more tears or suffering or pain or death. When my baby was born, I imagined the day when Dad will hold his grandson and we will all be together again. My baby will have an eternity full of perfect grandfather memories!"

What kind of memories would you leave your children or grandchildren if you died today? When Ben and Darlene's grandfather died he left behind a legacy of memories that will carry them through a lifetime. And he did it in a creative way.

A few months before his death, Grandpa rented a video recorder and recorded several hours of himself just sitting and sharing his life with the family. On the tape Grandpa shared from his heart those things that were important to him. He talked about the day he met Ben and Darlene's grandmother for the first time and how the first few years of their marriage were difficult. Tears came when he talked about burying their firstborn son in infancy and what it was like to lose a good wife.

Grandpa talked about God and how he had gone through times of doubt. He told about how God had become more real to him since Grandma was gone and how he looked forward to seeing her again in heaven.

When he finished the tape, Grandpa made several copies and gave them to all the grandchildren. It was a legacy for his loved ones and a gift of love to generations he would never see.

NOTES

1. Charles Sells, *Unfinished Business* (Portland, Oreg.: Multnomah, 1989), p. 162.
2. Adapted from Sells, *Unfinished Business*, pp. 161-62.
3. Gary Smalley and John Trent, *The Blessing* (Nashville: Thomas Nelson, 1986), p. 117.
4. Kevin Leman, *Measuring Up* (Old Tappan, N. J.: Revell, 1988), p. 23.
5. Susan Forward, *Toxic Parents* (New York: Bantam, 1989), pp. 217-18.

Part 3

Making the Most of Your Memories

9

FATHER MEMORIES AND
IMPROVED RELATIONSHIPS

My family and I settled back in our seats, anticipating a comfortable flight from Detroit to Dallas and then home to Tucson. As we approached Dallas, I pressed my face to the window, looking for the landing strip, and noticed a giant black cloud hanging over the airport. I wondered what the pilot was thinking—and was a bit nervous as he dropped the landing gear and started the the final approach to the field. Within moments we were surrounded by a whirl of wind, rain, lightning, and mean black clouds.

The plane was tossed like a toy in the storm. Empty cans rolled on the cabin floor and magazines slid past my feet from four rows up. Suddenly the wheels came up and the plane jerked upward, heading straight back into the storm. Fear ran through the passengers. Chatter turned to silence. Smiles turned to looks of concern. As an experienced traveler, I wondered if this was it—the final ride. I could picture it on the 6:00 P.M. news.

We climbed through the storm, tossed and jerked as though we were on a ride at the fair. I took inventory of my family. Each was responding differently. Evan, our firstborn, had his eyes closed and his hands folded together tightly. I could hear him praying, "Lord please let us land safely. I don't want to die in this stupid plane."

Our daughter, who was about seven, was casually looking around the plane to see what everyone was wearing and wondering why everyone in the cabin was so quiet. By this time my wife, Donna, was leaning into the in-case-of-illness bag. Then I looked over at our youngest son, Derek, whom we call D. J., to monitor his reaction.

Just as I turned I caught him, toy airplane in hand, exuberantly acting out his impression of a crash. He took the toy airplane and, making giant arching motions with his arm, pretended to crash the plane into his seat, complete with sound effects. Then, much to the horror of the lady to his left, he looked at me with a little grin and asked at a level the pilots could have heard, "Are we going to crash and catch on fire?"

FATHER MEMORIES PREDICT THE RESPONSE

Things settled down after the pilot directed the plane to another landing field. As I thought about the way my family responded to the crisis, I realized that I could have predicted what they would do because I know their behavior patterns. How well can *you* predict the actions and attitudes of the people around you? You may not understand or communicate well with those you work with, sit next to in church, or even live with. Father memories can help you know better all those you interact with and can help you anticipate how they will respond in future situations.

Consider how father memories might help us respond wisely in the following settings.

- John is the manager in a plant in our town. He is responsible for hiring and firing all staff. He told me once that one of his greatest frustrations is trying to pick the right person after only one or two interviews. "People almost always look good during an interview," John commented. "Even references aren't all that trustworthy because people slant them to be kind—not completely accurate. I wish I had another tool to help predict how people will get along on the job after they are hired."

  The father memories of those he was interviewing would be helpful to John. Hidden in them would be indications of how the interviewees would likely respond to authority, interact with others, and react under stress.

- Getting a word out of some teenagers can be frustrating. Many teens have difficulty telling you candidly how they view life, you, others, or God. Even coming in the back door of their life can be difficult. As the parents of one teenager said, "I wish I could understand how and what she is thinking. I don't know what values are shaping her decisions, so it's hard to trust that they will be good choices."

  Father memories could be a window to that teenager's world, as you will see from the example of Steve later in this chapter.

- Rod and Barbara are caring for Rod's aging mother. Barbara wants it to work but says, "I just don't understand my mother-in-law. She is so different from my own mother."

  As Barbara and her mother-in-law began to talk about their father memories, a new level of cross-generational understanding emerged.

Janet and Chris have been married for just over a year. It is a second marriage for both. Since I had counseled with each of them before their marriage I knew them quite well. So I was concerned when I heard of Chris's decision to take a new job fifteen-hundred miles away.

Chris had father memories filled with action and adventure, so I could have predicted that when the opportunity presented itself for an exciting new position he would go for it. The problem is, he never talked the move over with Janet. The father memories Janet had shared made it easy for me to anticipate her response, though apparently Chris had never considered them.

Janet is a firstborn who remembers her father as a strong, stable leader. She recalls: "Every Saturday morning Dad would get up at 7:00 A.M. and work on projects around the house until noon. Then, after lunch, he would wash the car and get it ready for a new week. He ran his life like clockwork." And so does Janet. The last thing Janet wants in life is to be blind-sided with a big move. So when Chris dropped the bomb, it blew up in his face.

I wasn't surprised. It was all in their father memories.

As you review the chart on the next three pages, think about a selected person's father memories. There will likely be variations on the general themes given in the chart as they relate to different memories, but the general predictions will help get you started. The chart is composed of samples of several father memory themes and accompanying predictions about the relationships involved. I have come across the themes I have listed consistently in my counseling sessions.

PAST	PRESENT
Main Theme in Father Memory	*Prediction About Relationship*
Anger	Anger is interfering in present relationships. That anger might show up only on occasion as an outburst or regularly in cross or harsh behavior. Control in relationships is important to you. You may experience frozen rage—indicated in depression and physical symptoms. You need to watch for resentment against males in authority—husbands, pastors, bosses, coaches, teachers, policemen, and government officials.
A critical father	Intimacy is difficult for you, as is trust. You may be trying constantly to measure up, struggling with the sense that no matter how hard you try the results will never be good enough. Procrastination is likely an issue with you. You tend to be hard on yourself and critical of others—including your critical father!
Indefinable emotion	You have difficulty identifying and understanding what you feel at certain times. You have trouble dealing with the emotions of others, and strong displays of emotion make you

PAST	PRESENT
Main Theme in Father Memory	*Prediction About Relationship*

	uncomfortable. It is hard for you to tell others what you feel, partly because you are not sure what you *do* feel and partly because you have been conditioned not to feel, but instead to bury or deny your emotions.
Feeling of fear	It is likely that you are overly cautious in relationships, cling to security, and avoid conflict. Risk taking and letting go is not easy for you. You have to resist the tendency to worry.
Feeling of embarrassment	You are a pleaser. Looking good to others is important to you, sometimes even too important, because you are likely to be overly concerned with what others think about you and your behavior. You are cautious. Self-consciousness sometimes interferes with your ability to socialize naturally.
The focus is on the family	Family relationships are important to you. You look forward to family gatherings and holidays, and you value time together doing things. Family priorities are near the top of your list.
Feeling respected	You expect respect and have self-respect. You value earning the respect of others and treating others with respect.

PAST	PRESENT
Main Theme in Father Memory	*Prediction About Relationship*
Lack of emotion	It is a struggle for you to express and understand your feelings. You either have strong emotions and are not sure what to do with them or you cannot nail down what you feel.
Wholesome humor	You have the ability to laugh at yourself and life. You have a good sense of humor and like to set others at ease by seeing the funny side of things as well as the mishaps.
Leisure and fun	You expect to enjoy life and your relationships. You know how to have fun and help others have a good time. Enjoying times together is important to you.

PUTTING FATHER MEMORIES TO WORK

Father memories can be used to avoid conflict, increase intimacy, and improve the quality of your life. To trip over a hole once is an accident. To trip over it daily is foolish. By studying your father memories you can discover the areas that will repeatedly trip you up in your desire for harmony and closeness. As you unlock secrets from your childhood you gain new insight into ways of working around the problem areas or dealing with issues to improve your relationships. Let's look together at how father memories relate to key relationships in life.

I AM NOT YOUR FATHER

Father memories will give you important information about how you and your spouse will complement one other and where you will conflict in your marriage, as we saw with Chris and Janet.

Donna and I were married as teenagers, which is generally not a good idea. Neither of us would recommend that our children marry that early. It was only by the grace of God, a lot of hard work, and supportive friends and family that we have a strong marriage. Fortunately, we were wise enough to wait eight years to have children.

When we look back twenty years we realize now how much we didn't know about loving each other. Fortunately, we came from similar backgrounds, as our childhood memories reveal, which helped smooth out the adjustment phase of our marriage. However, there are still areas in which we see things differently.

Because of what she remembers her father doing, my wife has the strange idea that men should like to work in the yard. Donna believes, therefore, that I should enjoy working side by side with her in the backyard garden. If not in the garden, then at least the flower bed. Thanks a lot, Dad-in-law!

On the other hand, I think dirt should stay on the outside while I stay inside. My father memories do not include men working in the yard or dirtying their hands in a manure pile for the sake of plump potatoes or beautiful begonias. It is easy to see that the origin of this conflict about one of my roles as a good husband has nothing to do with my personality or preferences. Donna's expectations are based upon her father's behavior—which is not standard or mandatory for all husbands.

Pardon the pun, but as I often tell her, "I never promised you a rose garden."

It was important for us to talk through our differing expectations and work out compromises. Donna and I found other areas in our father memories where we complemented each other. Those areas of agreement showed up in our fathers' values, priorities, commitment to Christ, and Christian service. As you review your own father memories, look carefully at little things that irritate you, especially as they relate to such significant issues as

- money
- time management
- family priorities
- sexual views
- friendships
- church

Just talking through the differences in your opinions in a non-threatening way and discussing the example your fathers set by their behavior in those areas can be freeing. If you identify areas of potential conflict, don't stop there. Talk through some compromises or changes on both your parts that will help you deal with the conflict areas and bring you closer. It may be best to work on a minor area of disagreement first, then move to more emotionally charged issues.

With the support of your spouse, you may also be able to mend some areas in your relationship with your father. If you determine it would be best to have a heart-to-heart talk with your dad about your father memories, make certain that your father knows that you love him and that he's not on trial. Tell him he is not meant to be perfect and that you are only trying to heal and improve the relationship. The tone and preparation for the setting will affect the outcome and ease his or your tendency to become defensive or offended.

Try to focus first on those issues that are the clearest in terms of objective "evidence," which is to say events in which the details are least disputed. That way you and your father will at least agree on what happened. If your father intimidates you or refuses to validate any of your feelings, have your spouse back you up in a non-threatening way, but don't let the discussion degenerate into an argument.

THE WORLD THROUGH YOUR CHILD'S EYES

If you really want to know what your children are thinking, ask them to share their father memories. When I asked my teenage son, Evan, he remembered my taking him over to Donaldson Elementary School to play catch. My daughter, Andrea, recalled that I sang a little made-up song to her that was a take-off of the song "My Girl." But to add entertainment value, I always dragged out the phrase My-y-y-y Girl-l-l-l. Both memories appear positive, right?

Not necessarily. When Andrea recounted the father memory she added the note that she always felt a little embarrassed when I sang the song. Her comment helped me see life the way she sees life. I learned that she likes to be with Dad, but she doesn't want to be embarrassed because of me. The message was "Be careful with my feelings and don't draw too much attention my way."

You can take a clock apart to find the mechanism that makes it tick, but it's not so easy with children. Yet we parents want to know what's going on inside our kids. We want to understand how our children feel and why they behave the way they do. No parents I know want their children to turn out to be failures morally, financially, or relationally. All of us want the best for and from our children.

As good parents we work, plan, and pray that our children will grow to become mature, responsible adults. Some parents appear to just cross their fingers and hope for the best. Others use proved methods of communication and parenting. The bottom line is to develop a good relationship with your children while helping them to become mature and responsible adults—whole people full of love and integrity.

Once when Josh McDowell and I were speaking together at a parenting conference on the East Coast, I heard him make this insightful observation about parent-teen interaction:

"Rules without a relationship cause rebellion."

Beating children over the head with rules, regulations, and expectations is not the way to lead. Authoritarian parenting has negative results in the long run. Barking out orders may fit the military style, but it falls far short of God's design for parenting. Yet permissiveness misses the mark as well and can be very damaging also. The key is to be an authoritative parent, helping children live under your authority, without becoming an authoritarian parent who rules over others with little respect for them or regard for their feelings. Authoritative parents set loving limits and hold children accountable. Kevin Leman and I call it "reality discipline."

Once when I was leading a father memory seminar a seventeen year old raised his hand, wanting to share his father memory. I walked down the aisle to hand him the microphone and encouraged him to share what he remembered. Steve introduced himself as he stepped into the aisle next to me and then went on to say, "I have a very vivid memory of my father from when I was about five years old. He was teaching me to ride a bike. I remember that he was holding onto the seat and ran along next to me as I tried to ride. Whenever he let go I would go off the sidewalk and fall. I was really scared, but as long as my father held onto the seat I felt OK."

I asked Steve if he knew the significance of that little father memory. "Not really," he responded. I started to say, "Let me tell you what I see," but before I could do so I was interrupted by a man sitting in the second row.

The man jumped to his feet and blurted out, "Let me tell him what it means—I think I know." Somewhat taken aback by his boldness, I told him to go ahead. "Steve, you're afraid to venture off on your own away from your family, aren't you?"

"Ah, I guess I am," Steve replied.

"Are you waiting for your dad to give you a push and some encouragement so that you can get along out there in the world on your own?"

"Yeah, I suppose," Steve echoed again.

By this time I was interested in the intensity of the discussion going on between young Steve and this man across the room. The man noticed my quandary and explained, "The reason I spoke up is that Steve is my son. That father memory confirmed what I've been wondering for some time."

That was one of those "Ah-ha! So that's it!" moments when the pieces of the puzzle came together in an instant. Later in the day Steve's dad told me, "When Steve shared that memory about the bike it was a turning point in our relationship." Up to that time the two of them had been dancing around the topic of Steve's impending graduation and move out of the house. There had been little discussion, and, as Steve put it, "It was difficult for me to talk to my dad about my fears."

That's the point. When your child recounts a father memory, he or she is cutting across the parent traps that often shut down communication. Your child will share his inner self with you through his father memory without knowing how much the memory and perception reveals of his true nature.

You and your child can use information gained from father memories for many purposes. The five most important I have experienced in my family counseling are the following:

1. *Father memories help siblings understand one another better.* Recounting father memories will help siblings communicate among themselves at a deep level. It will make them more aware of their differences and similar-

ities. It is especially interesting to note how children from the same family recall the same event in totally different ways. So remember, no one's version of what really happened is "right" and someone else's version "wrong." Keeping that perspective will help to reduce sibling rivalry and quarrels.

2. *Father memories help children understand themselves better.* Especially during the adolescent years, any increase in self-understanding is a useful tool. Father memories can help teenagers interpret who they are and what they truly value. That can be a meaningful way for your child to bypass peer influence and get to the basics of his personality and priorities. Father memories will help your child appreciate his or her uniqueness and sense of belonging apart from the pressure to be like the rest of the adolescents in his group.

One of our son Evan's earliest memories was a real eye-opener for him and for me. He recalls, "I was sitting on a swing out in the backyard. A woman walked by, and I thought she was my grandma. I called out to her and she turned—but it wasn't Grandma. I felt embarrassed."

Like father, like son. That could easily have been one of my own memories. It represents something in Evan's life he wants to change. As I told him of similar themes in my own memories ("I felt stupid"; "I felt embarrassed") and the lies that have influenced me because of them, Evan could see the negative messages at work in his life. As we prayed about it and worked at correcting his thinking, Evan and I both felt better about his perception of that memory. It was a positive experience for us.

3. *Father memories help children understand their parents.* Recounting your own father memories can break down walls and begin the process of open communication. As your children come to understand more about the home in which you grew up, they will gain new appreciation for your character strengths and weaknesses. Give them every opportunity to get to know you better.

As I mentioned when we talked about understanding your father's father memories, it can also be a bonding experience for your children to hear their grandparents sharing their early childhood recollections.

4. *Father memories can help children make career choices.* Characteristics seen in father memories can be helpful information to consider in making a choice of college or career. Was your son happiest as a child when he was creating something or thinking up ways to make something work? Maybe engineering or other technical fields would be a good fit. Was your daughter always doing something with someone in her memories? If so, it might be wise for her to shy away from loner careers, such as research science or freelance writing or positions requiring extensive travel. Look for father memory themes that indicate your child's deepest interests, abilities, and strengths.

5. *A parent can use his children's father memories to make himself a better parent.* Each child is unique and should be treated as an individual. To be successful at parenting you need to know how you can best teach and support each particular child. Father memories provide the clues. In addition to other things we've previously mentioned, ask yourself the following questions about the memories your child reports:

- How am I as a parent characterized in the father memory? What does that indicate about our relationship?
- How have I contributed to my child's seeing life the way he or she does?
- If my child continues to view life this way, how could it affect him or her in the future—both positively and negatively?
- What is one thing I can do to help my child improve his or her perception of life, me, or God?
- Does the father memory reveal any hurt that I am responsible for—and if so, have I asked my son or daughter to forgive me?

Understanding is the first and most important step. The more you understand yourself and each other the better prepared you will be to deal with conflicts or opportunities for closeness in the future. I would encourage every family to take time to discuss each other's father memories. Make it a fun setting, perhaps sitting around the dinner table while you are on vacation or perhaps while you are looking through the family photo album. Recounting childhood memories is a great place to start making more good memories!

TAKE THIS JOB AND LOVE IT!

Picking the wrong person for a job can be a costly mistake. I use father memories as part of the interview process to help me understand how a potential employee would fit in with my staff. So can you.

I look for a good match between what is required of the person in the job and what I see as strengths in his father memories. If the job requires a lot of detail work, I will be looking for someone who thinks in detail—and I'll see that in the father memory. If it's a team player I need, I look for such words as *we* or *together* or indications of cooperation on activities. If the position requires long hours and the father memory shows a strong attachment to family, it is essential that I clarify the job description and time commitment up front to eliminate future conflict. Likewise, a person whose father memory shows enthusiasm for challenges and new experiences is not a good bet for a job that offers a stable but monotonous daily routine.

As a male authority figure, I am interested in the chemistry between the job applicant and his father as shown to me in the father memory. If the father memory indicates that the applicant and his father had a healthy, close relationship I breathe easier as a boss. If the father memory indicates constant friction, mistrust, deceitfulness, or rebellion I'd best beware. I don't want to hire someone to repeat past mistakes on company time. Father memories are just one of many criteria for hiring, but I never leave them out.

At this point some of you may feel that I'm jumping to the conclusion that people can't change. Not so. But I agree with savvy businessman Harvey Mackay, author of *Beware the Naked Man Who Offers You His Shirt.* Mackay writes:

> There are certainly other ways of looking at things. Perhaps you've found that experience is the great teacher that helps you gain knowledge and avoid making the same mistake twice. Not for

me, nor for many others. Most of us are such creatures of habit, our mistakes are so ingrained, our character so locked into place, we aren't even smart enough to make new mistakes. We keep making the same dumb ones over and over again.

I figure if I only make the same mistake twice I'm ahead of the game. My rule is, never make the same mistake *three* times.[1]

As an employer I have found that it is a mistake to hire a person to fill a position that runs contrary to the themes found in his father memory. That is not to say that people cannot change—it is just that I don't want to reform them to conform with the job description.

Father memories work for self-evaluation, also. I try to consider my own disposition and abilities when I think about taking on a project. Like everyone else, I sometimes start to talk myself into things or to say yes to requests from others that really aren't right for me as a person. My father memories help me do some digging to see if I'm really suited for the task I'm considering. Is it really what I'm called to do, or is it more suitable for someone else?

BROTHERS, SISTERS, AND STEPSIBLINGS

Adult siblings can be as different as night and day. If the first-born is punctual and all business, the secondborn might enjoy racing from one project to the other on a flexible agenda. Baby Tommy might be a ham who enjoys a good laugh more than a good deed. In most families differences in personalities, preferences, and lifestyles are obvious. As I have already said, brothers and sisters from the same family are not created equal. Those variables create tension, and, for the sake of family unity, the equation has to be adjusted.

When Susan and her brother Donald first started working together in the family business, all was fine. But as time passed, their temperaments began to clash. Susan wanted order and stability, whereas her brother aimed for rapid growth and expansion of the business. Those goals were not compatible, and soon the siblings were clashing on small, daily office decisions.

As we talked, I asked them both to recount a father memory or two. Predictably, the memories they chose were completely different. But through the exercise of reporting those memories, each had the opportunity to experience the world the way the other sibling perceived it. They became more willing to appreciate each other's uniqueness and valuable contribution to the business.

Then, while they were openly communicating with one another, we ironed out some guidelines to smooth out the business dispute. We discussed practical details, such as who would have power and control over which areas. And we put money matters into print. It was important to Susan's security and the company's well-being to determine exactly how much cash would be designated for the operating fund, backup savings, and expansion of the business.

If you are having difficulty understanding or getting along with one of your brothers or sisters, turn to his or her father memories. From those memories you may gain the insight you need to deepen an existing relationship or to mend a damaged one. Don't stop with the father memories. Build on what you learn, and determine practical action steps you can take to make things better in the future.

Don't be surprised if your recollections vary greatly. Ron, the oldest son in a farming family, remembers the first harvest after they bought a new farm as being a time of exhaustion and frustration. He recalls being angry at his dad for buying more land and making him work so hard. Ken, on the other hand, the youngest boy in the family, remembers the same harvest as an exciting time filled with the fun of riding along in the field enjoying the activity. He remembers being happy because his dad was happy about the purchase of the new farm. The same event brought forth totally different emotional responses from the two brothers simply because they experienced it in completely different ways—and the details of what they recall will tend to validate their unique perceptions.

Comparing father memories among siblings is like hearing the five blind men describe an elephant. Each man described the part of the elephant closest to him. One described a tail like a rope, the next a body like a wall, and so on. They quarreled over who was right. But of course, all of them were right and none of them were right. In the same way, each sibling will describe an event the way he or she was touched by it, and everyone will see the story from a different perspective. Keep in mind that it's OK if your memories differ from those of your brothers or sisters.

To help you get started, here are some questions you and your siblings can answer together. Each sibling should recount a father memory until you find one all of you remember clearly. Then consider the following:

1. How do our recollections differ?
2. How are our recollections similar?
3. What emotion does each sibling attach to the memory? What part of the father memory does each sibling regard as the most significant?
4. How do our individual differences fit our personalities to-day?
5. Why do we see the world so much alike, or so differently?
6. What practical steps can we take, or compromises can we work out, that will improve our relationship to one another?

FATHER MEMORIES AND IN-LAWS

Getting to know the parents of your spouse is a respectful and loving thing to do. It says to your husband or wife, "I love you so much I want to know and understand your parents and the impact they had on your life."

If you are single and dating, I strongly recommend that you get to know your respective families before you go down the flower-strewn aisle to tie the knot. When you get married to that man or woman of your dreams you connect with the whole family, if not physically at least emotionally.

Your mate's personality was formed in large part as a result of your in-laws' early impact on his or her life. The more you understand your in-laws, the better you will understand your spouse. Talking about father memories can open up interesting discussions and help you improve your relationship with your spouse's family. Here are a few questions to direct the conversation:

1. What are some of the earliest memories each of you has of his father?
2. How do you think your dad's approach to parenting affected your own parenting style?

3. How do you think all of that impacted _____ (your spouse's name) as a child?
4. What would you have done differently in raising _____ (your spouse's name) if you knew then what you know now?

LASTING RELATIONSHIPS ARE POSSIBLE

With all there is to achieve in life, we forget that life is made up of relationships. Relationships have the most enduring impact. All of eternity is pictured as an ongoing, never-ending relationship with God and His children. From the time of creation, loving one another has been at the core of life, the very reason for living. Good relationships bring happiness and contentment. Poor relationships result in pain, bitterness, and frustration. With God's help, you can establish a strong network of loving, supportive friendships and draw closer to family members. Listening to and learning from one another's father memories is a great place to start.

Note

1. Harvey Mackay, *Beware the Naked Man Who Offers You His Shirt* (New York: William Morrow, 1990), pp. 22-23.

10

FATHER MEMORIES: YOURS, MINE, AND MARRIAGE

On our first date I took my wife, Donna, to a high school football game. It was a typical November night in Michigan. Cold. As the evening passed, the temperature dropped like a rock. I noticed that Donna was rubbing her hands together trying to keep warm.

She finally saw that I wasn't taking the hint, and leaned closer to tell me her hands were cold. I did the only logical thing I could think of—I told her to sit on them.

They used to call me Mr. Smooth.

If you are married, think about the first time you laid eyes on Mr. Wonderful or Miss Perfect. Think about your first date. Try to remember what it was that first attracted you to your mate. What was it about him or her that first made your heart miss a beat and caused you to want to be together again and again and again? His sense of humor? Her way with words? Maybe it was just the chemistry as your eyes met that first time across the room.

I have a secret for you:

> The very thing that attracted you to your spouse will probably be the rub between the two of you at some point in your marriage.

My friends Gary Smalley and John Trent made this same point in their book *The Two Sides of Love*. They observed that many "conflicts are caused by viewing another person's natural strengths as weaknesses."[1] In other words, our perceptions of one another are often rooted in our expectations and upbringing.

EXPECTATIONS AND FATHER MEMORIES

During my first sessions with Jeanine and Derek Swanson, I asked them to tell me what attracted them to each other. A boyish smile came across Derek's face as he told me about Jeanine's zest for life and enthusiasm for new adventure. "Jeanine was just what I thought I needed to spark up my life," he said. "She made me feel good when I was around her. I always looked forward to our next date."

Jeanine, too, was smiling as she talked about her first impressions of Derek. "He seemed so stable and sure of himself, which was something that really appealed to me," she recalled.

"That sounds like a pretty good start to me," I said. "So what went wrong?"

Quickly Derek shot back, "She just doesn't seem to have her feet on the ground, and frankly, she demands more attention and excitement than I'm able to give."

I turned to Jeanine and asked the same question. Even before she answered I knew the rub for her would be Derek's boring and unimaginative lifestyle. She immediately confirmed that that was so. "His feet are not only planted firmly on the ground, they're set in concrete! I thought I wanted his stability," she said, "but I think I ended up with an overdose."

Later, when we talked through their early father memories, specific personality differences jumped right off the page. If Jeanine and Derek had understood the implications of their father memories before the wedding, or if they had talked through their mismatched expectations of one another and the reasons behind those expectations, much of their heartache could have been avoided.

I recommend that dating couples talk about their father memories. Exploring father memories is also an effective tool for premarital counselors. If you see a pattern in a father memory that raises a red flag—anger, depression, abuse, disrespect, neglect—then you should move very slowly in the courtship.

If you have been married for a few years, perhaps you've experienced the same sort of thing—the unique characteristic that made your spouse stand out above the rest became the point of friction in the marriage later on. Can you relate to any of the items in the chart below? If not, come up with your own list. If you need help getting started, refer to the chart in chapter 5 that listed good qualities that can become irritations if taken to the extreme.

What attracted you to your spouse:	*After the marriage comes the rub:*
His or her sense of humor	He or she isn't serious enough
His or her stability	He or she is boring and refuses to take risks
His or her good looks	He or she is too concerned with appearance and fashion
His or her generosity	He or she wastes money
His or her hard work	He or she is a workaholic
His or her sensitivity	He or she is moody or touchy
His or her imagination	He or she lives in dreamland
His or her money	He or she is preoccupied with finances and net worth
His or her charm	He or she isn't genuine
His or her education	He or she is a know-it-all

UNDERSTANDING MARITAL DISAPPOINTMENT

I explained to Derek and Jeanine that before disappointment in marriage can be dealt with a couple needs to know what the underlying issues are. The issues for the Swansons turned out to be the same as for most couples:

Marital disappointment = Unmet marital expectations

Disappointment isn't an incurable disease. As we talked, the Swansons began to see that there was hope for their marriage. They settled back into their chairs and seemed more relaxed than when they first came in. It was clear that Jeanine was forcing issues to the surface by insisting upon counseling because she was extremely disappointed with the state of their marriage and family life. On a positive note, her disappointment also fueled a desire to change things for the better.

This young couple, like many who have unrealistic expectations of one another, had been star-struck with high hopes for a happily-ever-after life. They jumped into marriage without taking a good look at the landing spot. Then they landed in a puddle of problems. To help Jeanine and Derek understand the extent and nature of their marital difficulties they needed a short course on the relationship between father memories and marital disappointment.

But first, they needed to understand what makes a marriage work. I told them that couples report that the three most important ingredients in marital satisfaction are

> friendship in marriage;
> agreement over priorities, goals, and values;
> commitment to the marriage.

Derek and Jeanine were strong on number three, but they needed to work on numbers one and two. As a Christian couple, the Swansons agreed that divorce wasn't an option, and they wanted me to help them put their marriage back together. I applauded them for their decision to work hard at preserving their marriage and encouraged them to focus on their priorities, goals, and values, as well as putting friendship back into the picture.

As we talked, I explained that the typical engaged couple can't even begin to imagine not having their needs met by the man or woman who brought such joy into their lives during dating. Most dating couples wrongfully believe that their mate will always supply a never-ending stream of satisfaction like an underwater spring bubbling forth satisfying, cool water.

So when the honeymoon is over and the stream dries up or sputters inconsistently, confusion, frustration, and anger set in. When that happens some people start to look for a new stream. Others try to live with their negative feelings and resign themselves to being miserable. A few courageous people confront the problem and deal with it directly.

Think through the questions below honestly to check the contentment level in your own marriage.

How Disappointed Are You?

1. I sometimes question if I should have ever married my spouse.

   ___ Yes   ___ No

2. My spouse doesn't measure up to what I expected before we got married.

___ Yes   ___ No

3. My mate really doesn't understand me.

___ Yes   ___ No

4. Our marriage is weaker today than it was a year ago.

___ Yes   ___ No

5. Others think our marriage is stronger than it really is.

___ Yes   ___ No

6. My spouse thinks our marriage is stronger than I think it really is.

___ Yes   ___ No

If you didn't score so well (three or more yes answers), don't lose hope. God's desire is for two people to live in understanding with one another. Even though you can't change your spouse, you can learn to understand him or her better.

It's All in the Father Memories

During my counseling session with the Swansons I explained how marital expectations can be extracted from father memories. After we had spent some time talking about the way father memories work, Jeanine jumped in with an insightful comment. "In other words, for me as a woman my father memories represent my personal view of men and therefore my relationship with Derek," she remarked.

"There's a close linkage," I responded. "And for you, Derek, father memories are snapshots of what masculinity is all about to you."

For the Swansons, as it can be for you, exploration of father memories was the beginning of a greater understanding of one another and thus a better marriage. Insight was the first step toward change.

After getting basic information about their families and their birth order within their families, I asked Derek and Jeanine to think back to their childhoods and tell me what they remembered. "So who wants to go first?" I asked.

Jeanine volunteered and reported the following stories from her past:

> I remember one day when I was about four or five years old, my mom and dad took me out to lunch all by myself. Usually when we went out it was with the entire family, including my two brothers. But this time it was just the three of us. And I remember feeling special and loved. It was great to have all of that attention pointed at me.
>
> Another father memory that comes to mind involves just my dad and me. We were riding along in the car, and I remember asking him why the sky was blue sometimes and then red and yellow other times. My dad took the time to explain how God had created the sunlight to change color as it goes through various angles as the light moves through the clouds or dust in the air. This particular memory stands out to me because I always enjoyed talking to my dad about that kind of stuff. I remember how good it felt to have my dad's attention and time.

As Jeanine talked I wrote down every word she spoke because the words she used and the emotions she attached to them would be the key to Jeanine's understanding her personal expectations for Derek.

If you have not already done so, take a moment to ask your spouse to recount some father memories. Write the memories down exactly as he or she states them. Then be your own psychologist and consider what expectations for marriage are hidden in those memories. What can you glean from the memory about your spouse's concept of the roles of men and women? What life themes do you see? Where do your spouse's memories clash with your own childhood experience? Don't be afraid to share both good and bad.

Your spouse's father memory _____

_____

His or her personal role _____

_____

The emotion attached to the clearest part of the memory _____

_____

The expectations of marriage you can see in the memory _____

_____

Here are some typical themes you might look for.

"I feel valuable, happy, and loved if . . ."

    I'm taking big risks
    Somebody is taking care of me
    I'm in control of myself and others
    I'm pleasing others
    I stay out of conflict
    I make a lot of money
    I look good to others
    I can escape or avoid my problems
    Everything seems safe and secure
    I'm active and achieving
    I'm alone pursuing what I enjoy

For Jeanine, the messages from her father memories were "I feel more valuable and better about myself when I receive security, affection, and time from Derek. I want to talk with him and enjoy his undivided attention." It was clear from her memories that family was extremely important to her, as was the need for the man in her life to be a good listener and affirmer.

Both of the capsules from her childhood involved doing something with someone she cared about. Doing something special together was the way to win Jeanine's heart. Detail was also evident in her father memories. She told us in the first memory that she was an only daughter. This was a tip-off that Jeanine is an orderly person and a hint that she was unrivaled as Daddy's little princess.

If Derek had had this information when he married Jeanine, he wouldn't have been so surprised that she had high expectations for him. He would have known that she expected him to

> give her lots of security and stability along with affection
> put marriage and family first
> like to talk with her and be the understanding listener her dad
>   was
> keep their marriage full of surprises and action
> be concerned about order

But since Derek was oblivious to those expectations, handsome prince or not, he was about done in. He had thought that Jeanine would do the giving and meeting of needs. He had not realized, let alone lived up to, the unspoken expectations she had of him.

As Jeanine and I talked about her expectations of Derek, I glanced over to see how he was taking it. The more Jeanine and I talked, the more uncomfortable he looked. After a minute or two he said to Jeanine, "I didn't know you expected those things from me—you never said anything."

Not wanting the discussion to focus only on Jeanine's expectations, I turned to Derek and encouraged him to recount his early father memories. As you read the memories he reported, keep in mind that they represent his personal picture of masculinity.

> Nothing really profound comes to my mind. My father was seldom around. In fact, when I think about my childhood what I remember most is me playing all alone in my bedroom. I felt rather comfortable as a child spending a lot of time playing by myself. I remember sitting in my bedroom one day making a little town out of some Lincoln logs.

Shifting his weight while glancing toward Jeanine, Derek recalled another early childhood experience:

> The only other father memory I can think of right off is of looking out my bedroom window and watching my father working in the backyard. Part of me wanted to go out and work with him and an-

other part of me was content to stay in my room to finish what I was doing.

I turned to Jeanine and asked her what she heard in Derek's memory. She gave him a little smile and said, "Now I see why you like to spend so much time alone. Even though it bugs me to death, I can see from those memories that being by yourself is your idea of a good time . . ." Then her voice quivered as she added in a whisper, "But where does that leave me?"

Looking to Derek, I said, "The thing that jumps out to me is a picture of you looking out your bedroom window and wondering if you should go or stay inside, while I see Jeanine outside the window waving at you to join her in this thing called life."

Neither Jeanine nor Derek was deliberately choosing to be self-centered in his approach to marriage. Are any of us so different?

1. *We decide early in life how we fit into the family.* For Jeanine, togetherness, activity, and conversation made her feel valuable. For Derek, it was being left alone to amuse himself with projects he enjoyed.
2. *We act out those beliefs as adults.* Jeanine was striving for Derek's time, involvement, and affection, whereas Derek was reverting to the pattern of spending time alone without too many demands.
3. *We want the other person to change to meet our needs.* Derek wanted Jeanine to give him more space and not be so demanding, whereas Jeanine wanted Derek to come out of his shell and pour more of himself into their relationship.

AT HOME WITH JEANINE AND DEREK

It all comes home to roost when the door closes behind you. After the honeymoon the reality of routine life settles in, perhaps in sharp contrast to individual expectations.

In *Your Inner Child of the Past* Hugh Missildine points out that marriage involves four people, not just two. It's the two of you along with the "inner child" that resides within you both.[2]

Jeanine's father memories revealed a woman whose picture of marriage was of living in a house surrounded by a white picket fence and a small garden out back where she and her husband could immerse themselves in deep conversation while planting petunias. With great regularity her husband would sweep her off her feet and take her away on spontaneous and exciting adventures.

What Jeanine got instead was a fifteen-year-old, used mobile home set out back of her in-laws' farmhouse, parked next to a rusted John Deere combine. During most of his nonworking hours, Derek wasn't out in the garden or sprucing up the place but was locked away in the extra bedroom working on his model airplanes or napping. As for those spontaneous surprises—they came in the form of previously unmentioned Sunday afternoon dinners with the in-laws. When it came to meeting Jeanine's need for intimacy, Derek didn't have a clue. As far as he was concerned, sex and intimacy were the same thing.

In short, Jeanine was in the midst of a rude awakening. Now that the sleep of romance had been rubbed away by the splash of reality, she could see clearly that she wasn't getting what she had expected. And what she was getting she didn't like. The marriage she had dreamed of was turning into a nightmare.

As you write out your own father memories and accompanying expectations for marriage, consider how they relate to marital disappointment. In my seminars I put the following formula up on the board as a guideline for spouses working together on their father memories:

> Most marital disappointment = The distance between marital expectations as seen through your father memories and the reality of what you get in the marriage.

For some people, such as Jeanine, the distance is more like the Grand Canyon than a crack in the sidewalk.

DON'T JUMP IN BEFORE YOU TEST THE WATER

If you are in a dating relationship and want to know the expectations and priorities of the other person, take a long look at his father memories. Look at the impact his father made on his attitudes, values, and behavior. Notice the interaction among family members, particularly how men and women are characterized in his father memories. Try to connect his present attitude toward his parents with his verbalized memories.

If you can pick out themes of open communication, respect for one another, time spent together, or any other ingredients of strong marriages, then discernment and good judgment will validate the quality of your relationship and potential harmony. But if you notice negative themes that your companion may be trying not to imitate but often slides into during unguarded or highly emotional moments, take time to reconsider the marriage.

Most people approach marriage with the best of intentions. People don't get married with the idea that it is not going to work. But conflicts do arise, and it is far better to part ways before the marriage than after, if it comes to that.

An exercise I recommend to people in a dating relationship is to put themselves into their companion's memory and see how it fits. I asked Jeanine to place herself in Derek's father memories as an observer. Like a mouse in the corner of the room, her job was to witness the world through Derek's eyes. As she did so, she could see what was important to him:

- playing alone, not joining the family
- looking out the bedroom window; passive, not active
- *I, I, I* every other word—no *we* anywhere

If the Swansons had completed this exercise before they married, the clash of expectations would have sounded like a cymbal in Jeanine's ear, muffling the sound of wedding bells. As it was, the clash of *I* versus *we, sitting* versus *doing, playing alone silently* versus *being together talking* created discord in their home.

Even so, it was not too late for Jeanine and Derek to make the changes needed to bring their married life into balance. They agreed on the following practical steps toward change:

- They would plan and complete at least one activity together each week. Talking through the plans was as important as the event itself and would not be left up to Jeanine.

- Derek would be allowed two evenings off, when Jeanine was free to meet her conversation and companionship needs by doing things with her girlfriends. Money would be budgeted for both his hobby and her outings.
- They would make an effort to bring new experiences into the marriage once a month—even if it was simply having Chinese food rather than hamburgers.
- Recognizing that the changes anticipated would be easier for Derek if he physically separated himself from his childhood home and familiar habits, the Swansons agreed to look for suitable housing in the small town nearby. That would make it easier for Jeanine to build healthy friendships and at the same time would allow Derek convenient access to the solitude of wide open spaces.

There were some rough times during the adjustment, but both Jeanine and Derek made great progress. In the same way, you can alter the pattern of behavior that conflicts with your marital expectations and satisfaction. Father memories will provide a major component of the elements you need to make those changes.

In a marriage, each spouse brings positive and negative baggage from his father memories to the union. If a couple gains insight from their father memories they can maximize each other's positives and minimize or correct the negatives. Father memories unlock secrets that deal with expectations and the quality of performance in marriage. Using insight gained from father memories to make practical adjustments will help create the healthy and fulfilling union God intended.

NOTES

1. Gary Smalley and John Trent, *The Two Sides of Love* (Pomona, Calif.: Focus on the Family, 1990), p. 29.
2. W. H. Missildine, *Your Inner Child of the Past* (New York: Simon & Schuster, 1963), p. 56.

11

WHAT DAD DID RIGHT

One former president of the United States has no recollection of ever learning how to read, but in his autobiography he does relate this interesting incident:

> I remember my father coming into the house one day before I'd entered school and finding me on the living room floor with a newspaper in front of me. "What are you doing?" he asked, and I said, "Reading the paper."
>
> Well, I imagine he thought I was being a bit of a smart aleck, so he said, "Okay, read something to me," and I did.
>
> The next thing I knew, he was flying out the front door and from the porch inviting all our neighbors to come over and hear his five-year-old son read.[1]

And young Ronald Reagan had his first opportunity to perform before an audience. Although his autobiography reveals that Reagan's home life included hard times and conflict, this snapshot shows one thing his dad did right. Whether or not you agree with Mr. Reagan's response, you will find in this memory an indication that Papa Reagan was interested and proud of his son's achievement. As he called attention to his little boy for doing something well, young Ronald must have been pleased. No doubt his self-confidence and self-esteem received a boost from the admiration and praise given by his father and neighbors.

And partially because of what his parents did right, Ronald Reagan developed strengths that served him well into the future. We shouldn't be surprised that the adult Ronald felt confident of his intelligence and ability to learn and felt comfortable on stage. When a key person believes in you as a child, as Reagan's father did, you generally grow up to believe in yourself when confronted with various trials and challenges in adulthood. When you begin life with a poor foundation from Dad a confident outlook is less likely.

CREDIT WHERE CREDIT IS DUE

What do you like about yourself? What character qualities are your areas of strength? What values and beliefs are most important to you? Chances are, as was true of former President Reagan, the seeds of your successes and strengths were planted in your childhood. This is a chapter set aside to help you recognize and applaud all that your parents, particularly your dad, did right.

When things go wrong in our lives we are sometimes quick to put the finger on Mom and Dad, figuring that if somehow they had done things differently we wouldn't have turned out the way we did or wouldn't be struggling with the problems we face. Some people spend time digging up the dirt of the past in order to sling mud at someone else. But as the saying goes, "He who slings mud loses ground!"

It is time to set the record straight and look at the positive impact of the parenting you received. Let us give credit where credit is due. Let us also be willing to look in all humility and honesty at our good side.

To get you started looking for the bright spots in your father memories, I'm going to list just a few of the significant skills you may have learned. Go through the list quickly and draw a line under those traits that are most important to you. Then move back through the words and put a plus by those that you actually possess. (You aren't expected to have them all, but try to give yourself an honest assessment without false modesty.) Finally, use the list below to put a check beside those you see in your father. Probe your childhood memories for hints of his modeling or training in those areas.

_____ **responsibility:** recognizing and doing your part
_____ **confidence:** feeling able to do it
_____ **initiative:** seeing what to do and moving into action
_____ **patience:** willing to wait when necessary
_____ **kindness:** showing caring concern for others
_____ **problem solving:** putting your knowledge and ability
               to use
_____ **integrity:** telling the truth and living out your convic-
               tions
_____ **teamwork:** working well with others
_____ **perseverance:** completing what you start
_____ **motivation:** wanting to do it
_____ **determination:** doing it when you don't want to
_____ **courage:** inner strength to act rightly in spite of fear
_____ **creativity:** coming up with new ways to say or do it
_____ **independence:** doing it on your own when neces-
               sary
_____ **supportiveness:** encouraging others to do their best
_____ **verbal:** able to express feelings and concerns
_____ **obedience:** able to respect and submit to authority
_____ **loving:** caring deeply for others

Wherever you find any of those traits in yourself, you have found the touch of God and the touch of love on your life. Often that touch first came through your father's hand or your mother's influence. You may have learned those and other skills as a child without even being aware you were learning them.

Sometimes fathers pass along more than just qualities. They transfer practical skills for daily life: teaching us how to change a tire, use a hammer, hang a picture on the wall, or pass a football. Some sons and daughters follow after Dad in apprenticeship style, learning his trade. The number of father-and-son or father-and-daughter businesses in operation indicate that many dad's provide on-the-job training. Many more teach their children how to work hard to provide for their families through their own example.

Fathers also pass along the keys to their children's success in more indirect ways. My older brother, Larry, for example, is a master carpenter—and he sure didn't pick that up from Dad! But Dad did instill the qualities that make for a good carpenter, such as initiative, detailed planning, and confidence. In fact, when I think about my brothers and me I realize that each of us got a different dose of our father's various qualities. But all of us were instilled with Dad's most dominant character strengths—responsiblity, creativity, and a concern for others.

Most likely you will also notice that many of your strengths reflect the interpersonal skills or character strengths of one or both of your parents. Those skills and strengths may have been inherited, or one or both of your parents may have worked hard to build them into your character.

For example, the ability to believe yourself to be a friendly person capable of developing close friendships and to feel good about making friends is often linked to having a father or mother who affirmed you as a likable person and openly said that you were fun to be around. According to Charles Cooley, one of the founders of American sociology, what you think of yourself is for the most part determined by what you think the most important person in your life thinks of you. The famous "Cooley's Looking-Glass Self" certainly rings true for small children, who form their first image of themselves largely from the primary relationships they form with significant others, most often parents.

THE FATHER DAD WAS CUT OUT TO BE

Checking off the areas of Dad's strengths can make you more aware of the fathering style that was uniquely his according to temperament, talent, and time availability. Or it can make you more aware of your father's flaws. But the assessment exercise was not designed to point out all that your father never was or the skills he never mastered. Now is not the time to pass judgment. Instead, it is a time for looking at the traits you picked up from your father's areas of strength as a positive heritage. It is a time for examining whether there were legitimate reasons that explain why Dad was unable to perform well in certain areas.

Keep your father expectations realistic. The absence of a trait doesn't necessarily mean your father wasn't teaching it. Maybe you weren't learning!

Bart Campolo, co-author with his famous father of *Things We Wish We Had Said,* made some interesting observations about his dad, Tony Campolo. Bart could have easily been intimidated by his father's expertise as a speaker and writer, or he could have been discouraged by his father's failure to take him camping or coach his Little League team. Instead, Bart comments:

> My father . . . is simply a human being with strengths and weaknesses, abilities and inabilities, gifts and flaws just like everyone else. What makes him so magnificent to me is that he has not been paralyzed by what he cannot do or overcome by what he does not have.
>
> Instead, my father has focused all of his energy on maximizing what he does have and realizing the potential of what he can do. He has played to his strengths, and he has won out by doing so. Tony Campolo is not good at everything, but he is undeniably great at being Tony Campolo.[2]

Allow your father the freedom to be himself. Don't expect your dad to be the type of father he was never cut out to be. His personality and background and abilities shaped his parenting style—regardless of your picture of the nonexistent perfect parent. All fathers are not created equal. They have different talents and temperaments. A responsible father, for example, may not have been a good team player. And a team player may not have been a good problem solver.

What your dad did right had to be right and fitting for him, as well as for you. If your father was quick-witted, quick-tempered, and quick to speak by nature, for example, you could waste your life waiting for a patient father who is a great listener. Or you could choose to look in other areas for the strengths of his particular parenting style.

As you look over the list above, don't ache wistfully over the sort of man your dad never was and never could be. As Bart Campolo put it, "I don't think that every parent could do what my father was able to do. In spite of all the 'how-to' books about parenting, people cannot create in themselves capacities that God has not placed within them. Fortunately, there are many ways to express love and to help children grow."[3]

As you probe your father memories, look for the times your father expressed his love and helped you grow using the methods that were natural to him. Your dad's unique fathering style may have some hidden benefits not found in "textbook" parenting. Maybe it is time tell your father, "Thank you for simply being you and always being there for me."

LOOK AT ME!

High on the list of things Dad can do right is found in the phrase *being there.*

Songwriters Bill and Gloria Gaither ask themselves, "What *did* our parents do right? According to Gloria, in *What My Parents Did Right,* "Bill always said that the most important thing his parents did was to always 'be there.' The way he said these two words suggested a great deal more than physical presence on a somewhat regular basis. He seemed to be saying that his parents were there for him in others ways, too: that they were there for emotional stability, for financial and spiritual undergirding, and for intellectual encouragement. 'Being there' also had a hint of an all-knowing surveillance and suggested consistent discipline that did not laugh at mischief one day and punish it the next."[4]

Throughout childhood, each of us cries out the universal request, "Look at me!" Little children want their parents to give them lots of attention, to watch over their progress toward success, and to share their lives. "Come see my puzzle—I did it all by myself!" "Daddy, look at me! I can ride a bike with no hands." "Mom, look what I made!"

Children want their parents to *be there* for them.

As adults, we usually do a good job of noticing babies, remarking with enthusiasm at each small triumph. We cherish the first smile. The first words. The first steps. But somehow, as the child grows we see less and less, and pretty soon we're not noticing much at all unless there's a problem. But even as the days went by in a blur of busyness, many dads did not miss the opportunity really to look at their children and appreciate them at each stage of childhood. Heartwarming memories such as those remind us that fathers are doing some wonderful things right. Christie recalls:

My father was very family-centered. He never chose hobbies that excluded us—he said he would have time for those things later. Dad was always there for us. I don't remember him ever missing a dance recital or softball game.

At the time I took it for granted, but now I'm amazed that a busy engineer could have made that much time for us—I understand more of the sacrifices it took on his part. I've shown my appreciation, a little late, with hugs and thank yous for the fond memories of times we shared. And I invite him often, so he can stay active in our family life. When he goes out of his way to be involved with my kids, I tell him what a great grandfather he is. We have a very good relationship.

THE ACCUMULATIVE EFFECT OF LITTLE

At this point some of you might be thinking, *But my father wasn't there for me. He was always so busy doing his thing that I was brushed aside.* OK. So you know your dad blew it by not spending more time with his kids, by being controlled by a sinful, addictive lifestyle, or by inflicting abuse. Now what?

If this is the case for you, I suggest that you try to look for the positive messages that *were* communicated through the little things. Not everyone can come up with extra-special memories of tenderness, affection, and love, but most people can find something good that came out of their childhood. Many of us harbor feelings of "I wish I had had Dad all to myself more" or "I wish he had known and understood me better." But that is life. You have to learn to make the most of any positive training you received and take it from there.

Often positive aspects in a father memory are overshadowed by negative feelings. Whenever Lee talked about his father it was in a critical tone: "I'm a military brat—all I can remember is moving from one town to the next. We never settled anywhere long enough to build deep friendships, and I really resented my dad putting us through that." Lee was obviously displeased with his father's priorities in life. And Lee might be right. But what is important for Lee, and you, to do at this point is to glean anything positive you can from your father memories. Lee's dad, for example, passed his son a heritage that included love of country, self-discipline, fidelity in marriage, and enthusiasm for life. But Lee permitted resentfulness to cloud the truth.

Maybe you can build on the sense of humor, work habits, or positive values you have picked up from your father. Values can come through in many ways—attitudes, talk around the table, things you did as a family—even if you spent little quality time alone with Dad. Values can be caught just by watching your father and noting his priorities.

When my clients have trouble naming anything Dad did right or coming up with something positive from their upbringing I often ask them to do a simple exercise. I have them write out the good things their family stood for and believed in. Here is a list of some of the values they have mentioned that may also be a positive part of your heritage. To get started writing out your own list, check the items below that were communicated to you through words or deeds during your childhood. You may think of other things your father did right or of values he passed on to you in addition to those listed here. That's great! The longer the list the better.

My dad was

_____ a good provider
_____ the spiritual head of our home
_____ the leader of our family
_____ an encourager
_____ consistent with discipline
_____ concerned about my well-being

My dad modeled or taught

_____ love and respect for your fellow man
_____ obedience to divine commandments
_____ self-discipline and self-control
_____ humbleness of spirit
_____ tenderness and compassion for those who hurt
_____ respect for authority
_____ wholehearted devotion to God
_____ love for your country
_____ family is important—stay true to each other
_____ be honest—follow through on what you promise
_____ enthusiasm for life

_____ helping others is more important than simply helping yourself
_____ whatever you do, give it your best

Each father has his own way of relating, reflecting the uniqueness and sometimes the deficiencies of his own background and
makeup. Every mother has different personal strengths. But chances
are, whatever their background, your mother and father communicated something worthwhile to you as a child. Those convictions
served as a foundation for your early development and a guide for
the challenges that came with adulthood.

Jill Briscoe, the author of more than twenty books, credits her
parents for modeling the values and priorities that enabled her to
become a vibrant Christian. "What did my parents do right?" Jill
writes, "First, my sister and I never had any doubts about the fact
that they loved us. Our parents—especially my mother—told us all
the time. They didn't buy us off, but rather they emphasized that
the best things in life (like love) are free. . . .

"My parents also instilled in us a sense of responsibility concerning our family name. We were taught that our behavior could
affect our good reputation, so it was important to live honorably
even when we were out of our parents' sight. What we did and
how we did it would reflect on them, and my love for them curbed
my wild ways during my teenage years. Since I became a disciple
of Jesus, living a life that honors His name has been easy for me.
It's not hard to know why."[5]

The strengths and abilities we can be thankful for in adulthood are often a reflection of the parenting we received, parenting
revealed in our early childhood memories. But sometimes we
don't appreciate Dad's wisdom until we grow up a little or have
children of our own—then our fathers somehow get smarter.

Yesterday I was talking to Jackie, a young college student. I
asked her about her father memories, and she responded, "That's
really interesting that you should ask about memories of my father.
Memories of my dad from when I was a child are totally different
now that I'm in college. All I can remember as a kid is my father
telling us we didn't have enough money to go on vacation, or buy
a new dress, or a hundred other things I thought I needed."

With a smile Jackie continued, "When I think about how childish my feelings were during that time in my life I feel embarrassed. I remember how upset I felt because my dad was such a tightwad, but, boy, are things different now." Jackie turned to look out over the University of Arizona campus and added, "I'm twenty years old now, and in my sophomore year of college. My dad is paying for tuition, room, and board. All those years when I thought he was being selfish he was thinking only of us, saving money to put all three of us kids through college—and I sure can't be upset about that!"

She ended by saying, "If I knew then what I know now my attitude would have been different. I should have trusted more in his willingness to act in my best interest. A few years and a little distance gave me a new perspective."

The parenting we received is not the determining factor in our lives. God is in charge. And our choices matter. We can choose to cultivate an attitude of gratitude for what Dad did right in raising us. We can choose to make the most of the heritage we've been blessed with to become the person God has called us to be. We are fortunate, indeed, if we had a father who gave us a good example to follow, but even if we did not, we have been given a perfect example in God Himself.

In the course of writing this book I have been forced to turn my eyes around and closely examine the relationship between my dad and me. I've discovered that each father-and-son or father-and-daughter relationship is unique. My relationship with Dad is unlike his relationship with my brothers. As the baby of the family, I was treated differently than Warren and Larry; expectations and pressures changed. By the time I came along Dad was older and living through another stage of life than when my brother Warren had been a child ten years earlier.

I am learning that my dad doesn't have to be perfect to be my dad. And I don't have to be perfect to be his son. Like most people, I could come up with a list of father faults—but I choose not to. Rather, I want to say, "Thanks Dad, for the father memories that reinforce the good stuff in life.

"Thanks for your courage in standing for godly principles; thanks for staying married to mother; thanks for providing food, clothing, and other things when I was young; thanks for instilling in my life a vision that looks beyond my own interests; thanks for the piano lessons even though I dropped out; thanks for encouraging me to further my education; but most of all, Dad, thanks for making God the center of our family."

Take time now to reflect on all the things your father has done on your behalf and the benefits you enjoy as a result of the things he did right. In the next chapter we will look at ways you can accentuate those positives, overcome the negatives, and take steps toward lasting change.

NOTES

1. Ronald Reagan, *An American Life: The Autobiography of Ronald Reagan* (New York: Simon & Schuster, 1990), p. 25.
2. *What My Parents Did Right,* ed. and comp. Gloria Gaither (Nashville: Star Song, 1991), p. 39.
3. Ibid., p. 42.
4. Ibid., p. 12.
5. Ibid., pp. 32-33.

12

Putting the Past Behind You

Following a radio interview on the topic of early memories, I had a few extra minutes to talk with the host, Michael Reagan, before he went on with his program. I asked him what his earliest memory was. Michael paused for a couple of seconds and then said, "I recall the day as a young boy when my big sister Maureen told me that I had been adopted." When I asked him how he had felt about that bit of surprising news he hesitated, then said, "Given away . . . I felt given away."

Those were not the words I expected to hear from the adopted son of former president Ronald Reagan. Since time was short Michael suggested, "Randy, let me send you a copy of my autobiography. It will fill in the blanks."

After receiving his book, I read with interest the emotion-filled story of Ronald Reagan's adopted, eldest son. Michael wrote what his early memory indicated: "I grew up convinced that my birth mother gave me away because she didn't love me and I was bad."[1] On the next page he went on to say, "It is only in the light of recent discovery that I have come to realize that my memory has been selfishly selective. My parents—birth as well as adoptive—were not villains."[2]

Michael subtitled the book "On the Outside Looking In." Maybe you can identify with his feelings. Although you may not have been adopted, you still may feel as though you are on the outside looking in, craving for belonging but never feeling accepted and loved. The hurts and misconceptions that grew out of your relationship to your father may have burned so deeply into your personality that change now seems all but impossible. When you hear that significant growth can still occur, it seems like a gift only for others, a present you'll never open.

Michael Reagan was able to challenge his childhood memories, and so can you. I wrote this chapter hoping you would join me in the freedom I have found from the lies rooted in my father memories. Your lies are different from mine, but they come from the same source—distorted childhood memories and a desire to belong. As you know by now, my father memories involve feelings of embarrassment and wanting to please others. Although some aspects of my memories are healthy, other aspects resulted in self-defeating thinking and insecurity. But I am finding lasting change and personal healing—you can too.

To begin the process of putting the past behind you, join me by following these steps.

1. *Don't pull away emotionally:* I'm thankful for a wonderful wife and good friends who help me out here.
2. *Flip the coin:* I'm discovering there's another side to my life story, including my father memories.
3. *Uncover the lie:* There is no need to tell myself that I'm stupid or have to please everyone—that's a lie.
4. *Accept the past for what it was:* In my case, it was pretty good, so thank you, Lord.
5. *Learn from your hurts:* In my memories there were lessons to be learned about better ways to handle feelings of embarrassment and rejection.
6. *Don't let your father memories define who you are:* I am more capable than I've told myself for years—and so are you.

In the sections that follow, we'll elaborate on each of the above steps. I encourage you to keep a pencil and notebook close by so that you can jot down your own specific applications.

Don't Pull Away

I was on a jammed flight between Michigan and Arizona this past week. As I observed the people around me on the plane my gaze fell on a bag of books at the feet of the lady sitting next to me. One seat over, next to the window, sat her husband, with his face behind the sports section of *USA Today*. The couple appeared to be in their forties, and each wore fashionable clothes, with gold watches, diamond rings, and genuine leather accessories.

As we flew along I couldn't help but notice that about every fifteen minutes or so the woman put down the paperback novel she was reading and picked up another. That caught my attention, so I asked her if I could see her books.

As it turned out, this attractive woman was reading from a bag of books on romance, sex, and how to find the right man. She was losing herself in a paperback world. All the while, her husband sat next to her, unaware of her lonely winter. Not once during the three hours I sat next to the couple did either one talk to the other. Each was lost in his own world. Disconnected. Alone.

Apparently the woman had found that some peace and pleasure could be found in books. They were a way of passing the time and vicariously filling her need for intimacy as she lived out a single-though-married lifestyle. She deadened the pain by escaping into the lives of the characters in the books she read. She was pulling away from pain and real people.

Pulling away from hurts is like running away from a car accident. You only delay and enlarge the consequences. Emotional escape is no solution, only a means for allowing your imagination to carry you away. The first step to putting the past behind you is to come out of hiding and face your problems head-on. You can never really run away—you carry a lasting imprint of your pain with you deep inside wherever you go. To hide is to live in a fantasy world—and dream worlds have a way of bursting like bubbles sooner or later.

As a pleaser I tend to deny my own feelings and concentrate on the feelings of others. That may sound very spiritual, but it isn't. That is because in the process of denying my feelings I am actually resisting being honest with others and end up pulling away from people. I lose, and so do those I care about. So I have made a point of being more direct in letting others know my feelings—and it's a great improvement.

Although this first step may be scary, I encourage you to move toward others. Here are three simple ways you can join me in resisting the inclination to pull away from people or deny significant issues:

- *First, keep a journal to clarify your thoughts and feelings.* Often your thinking and emotions are out of sync. In your head you know you shouldn't pull away, but in your heart you want to. List any activities, excuses, or circumstances you are hiding behind to avoid dealing with your past and your present decisions. Write out how you feel about current and past situations in your life. My journal reveals patterns of thinking and behavior, allowing me to focus on specific issues rather than vague problems.
- *Second, explore the behaviors and habits that enable you to pull away from people.* Be honest. The energy generated by the wound is often channeled into negative behavior, such as alcohol or food addiction, marital affairs, and cycles of compulsive behavior used as an escape. Sarcasm, passive silence, or feigned indifference are also negative methods of walling people out.

  Positive activities, such as reading, exercising, or community involvement, can also become ways of compensating for and hiding from problems. For example, you may be pulling away from the pain in your marriage by pouring yourself into being a good mother or a caring friend. Maybe you just get busier and work so that your business crowds out memories and present tensions you don't want to deal with.
- *Talk privately with a trusted friend, pastor, or counselor.* A friend may be more objective than you in cutting through denial and pretense and thus be more able to point out the real issues. As an accountability partner, he or she can help you follow through on the changes you want to make.

  It is vital that you define the problem in specific terms, not vague sentiments. For example, the lady on the plane might conclude, "When I feel left out of life, I lose myself in a book to feel better. I tend to isolate myself from others when they don't respond or I am depressed. Believing the lie that nothing will ever change and there's nothing I can do about it fuels my drive to hide from it all."

Harry, the president of a company with some two hundred employees, had a habit of playing one responsibility against another one to shelter himself from honest criticism. In a moment of self-discovery he concluded, "When I know I'm falling short, I make myself look better by saying that pressing responsibilities at home are temporarily affecting my performance at work, or pressing responsibilities at work are interfering with my performance as a husband and father—which is half true. In this way I avoid having to do better and facing my failure. That's how Dad deflected criticism, and I'm doing it too."

Once the dysfunctional response has been identified you can begin to work on changing your directing thoughts and avoidance behaviors. Don't just mow the dandelions, pull them out by the roots. Otherwise, new self-defeating habits will likely pop up just as fast as you cut the old ones out.

FLIP THE COIN

Just as there are two sides to every coin, so there are always two sides to your father memories—the truth and the lies, or misconceptions. Michael Reagan spent years focusing on only one side of the coin, the side that told him, "You were given away." He wasn't listening for the rest of the story. The other side of the coin said, "You were chosen, wanted, accepted, and loved by your adoptive parents."

Michael had been telling himself that he was unwanted and given away, whereas in reality he was also being received and welcomed. Michael writes, "I was three days old when I was adopted. Around four years ago, I received in the mail from Dad's former business manager a hundred dollar War Bond accompanied by a letter that said the bond was 'in celebration of your coming home.' The bond was bought on April 4, 1945, by Ronald Reagan for Michael Edward Reagan. Receiving that bond took me back forty years in time. I realized that my dad must have loved me dearly. If only I had known it during my childhood."[3]

Everything that has happened to you is locked away in your brain. But why do you only remember a few things or nothing at all? You don't simply forget what happened. That would be impossible, except in cases of disease or injury. Once an experience gets processed by the brain it is recorded in what is called a "memory trace," where it can be called back as needed. Each memory trace contains not only the memory of the event but also our perceptions of and emotional response to it. How memory actually works is still a mystery under study, but it is clear that you don't erase a memory even though you may block it out.

So if you're trying to manage your father memories by forgetting them, I would recommend a new approach. Flip the coin to see another side to your life story. Look carefully for information to offset any exaggerated, misinformed, or biased conclusions you may have reached about what happened. Ask yourself:

- Were there parts of the event in my memory that I might be misunderstanding or overemphasizing?
- Did my father really feel that way, or did I just assume he did, and read into his behavior according to my perception? We usually find what we are looking for, in the sense that looking for signs of rejection or looking for signs of acceptance in the same story will yield contrasting data.
- Can I see some good or positive aspect of the negative experience I remember? Maybe the positive side should play the predominant role. Take a good look.

Be aware that your feelings will often conflict with the facts or color your interpretation of them. There's no such thing as bare facts in a father memory—the facts always come dressed up in coordinating clothes that fit our scheme of things. Kim knew that her dad had died in an airplane crash when she was four. Intellectually she realized that the facts clearly indicated he was a passenger in the plane with no control over the accident. But emotionally, as a little girl Kim felt abandoned because her father never came home again. In the same way, if you flip the coin to look at your father memories from a new angle you may discover that your emotions have been distorting those memories.

It helped Kim to imagine seeing her father in the moments before the plane crash thinking about how much he loved his family and how desperately he wished he could return to them. When Kim was able to see that he would have been as emotionally devastated at the thought of leaving her as she was of losing him, it helped her to put things into perspective. She still had to live with the loss, but the overtones of feeling abandoned faded.

UNCOVER THE LIE

Michael Reagan writes of a reoccurring nightmare he had. In it his family is about to enter heaven—all except him. He writes, "The gates open, and I step aside to let my family precede me. Suddenly God steps in front of me, placing His burning hand on my chest. My son Cameron turns around. 'Come on, Dad,' he says impatiently and starts toward me. But God is still halting my progress. He turns his back to me and takes out my Book of Life from deep within his white robes. He opens the book and shows my family a page. His voice booms in my ears. "Michael Reagan is not allowed into heaven because he is illegitimate . . ."[4]

Michael Reagan uncovered the lie that being adopted proved him to be bad—less than acceptable. We know, of course, that adoption is a great gift for both the adoptive parents and the adopted child. As far as getting into heaven is concerned, the Bible clearly states that the admission requirement is faith in Jesus Christ, who forgives sin—with no regard whatsoever to the circumstances of one's birth.

Even so, the powerful lies we begin to believe early in life can continue to influence us until the cycle is broken. We live by our private logic, and it is essential that those thinking processes be reshaped by truth.

A lie I tell myself from my father memories is "Be careful and play it safe—that's the way to live." I catch myself passing that message along to my children. For example, the other day I was watching my ten-year-old daughter, Andrea, walk through the living room with a pair of scissors in her hand. She was on her way to her room to finish up some homework projects. As she passed by me the words just leaped out of my mouth, "Be careful with the scissors—don't poke your eye out." My wife looked up from her work and said to me, "Why would she want to poke her eye out?" I immediately realized how ridiculous my words had sounded to a fourth-grader and caught the connection with the you-can-never-be-too-careful lie I associate with my father memories.

Without a conscious effort to break the cycle of those thoughts, the lies and their consequences will continue. Can you identify any lies that you tell yourself from your father memories? Maybe something like:

- The world only likes the beautiful people, and since I'm ugly I'll never really fit in—that's a lie.
- My father rejected me as a child; therefore he will reject me now—that's a lie.
- My father always complimented me for being obedient; therefore, to get along in marriage and in life I need to be compliant and fit into everybody else's plans—that's a lie.
- When I got A's in school my father was really proud of me; therefore, the way to win approval and acceptance is to get all A's in life and achieve excellence in all classes—that's a lie.
- My father always told me that I was the strong one in the family; therefore, I need to be the one to hold everything together and not let down—that's a lie.

Even in the most encouraging families, father memories can be distorted. Praise and encouragement can be interpreted by the child to mean that the performance is more important than the person. Children are great tape-recorders but lousy interpreters. Quite often the things that were said by our fathers were never meant to sound the way they did or to be understood the way we took them. Or our dads did things that turned out differently from what they had intended. Check carefully for misunderstandings that have resulted in incorrect messages in your memory bank.

ACCEPT THE PAST FOR WHAT IT WAS

A friend of mine, author and speaker Barbara Johnson, says that she carries a windshield wiper when she speaks "to use as a reminder that we have to wipe away the past."[5] The most effective way to wipe away the power we give the past is to accept the past for what it was. Here are some guidelines for the acceptance process:

1. *See your father memories for what they are.* Remember that they represent your personal view of life. You gave them significance, and you can let the air out of their inflated messages. It's your choice. You take away their significance by changing what you tell yourself.

   The first time Jody experimented with wearing makeup her dad happened to walk into the room. When he saw her less-than-professional attempt to look womanly, he grinned a little and shook his head. Her father didn't mean to be unkind or to imply that Jody would never be an attractive woman, but that's how Jody interpreted his behavior. She told herself the exaggerated lie, "Dad thinks I look funny and might as well give up on looking pretty—and he's right." Of course that was nonsense stemming from Jody's shaky adolescent view of her femininity. Her father had told her how pretty she looked on many occasions. Jody had to go back to the memory and accept her father's grin for what it was, simply a good-natured response to some lopsided lipstick!

2. *Commit your father memories to God.* The Bible says, "In everything, by prayer and petition, with thanksgiving, present your requests to God. And the peace of God, which transcends all understanding, will guard your hearts and minds in Christ Jesus" (Philippians 4:6-7). God can give you inner peace about your past and strength to face the future as you pray about the impact of your childhood memories.

   God sent His Son Jesus Christ to free us from the bondage of sinful life—including the hurtful stain of painful father memories. There is a great passage in Isaiah that says of Jesus, "The Lord has anointed me to preach good news to the poor. He has sent me to bind up the brokenhearted, to proclaim freedom for the captives and release from darkness for the prisoners" (Isaiah 61:1). If you feel like a captive to your past, remember that Christ has come to comfort you and set you free. You can claim your freedom from bad memories.

Think about the healing process as a partnership. God provides healing grace and power. But you must supply a willingness to change, face reality, and be obedient to God's Word.

3. *Forgive yourself and others who have wronged you.* A theme that runs through the heart of this book is the need to forgive, not merely to pretend to forget. As long as you are determined to get even or punish someone who hurt you, the past will never be put behind you.

Every year my wife and I attend the National Religious Broadcasters meeting in Washington, D.C. More than three thousand delegates come from around the world. Last year we were invited to have dinner with Joni Eareckson Tada. Joni is a paraplegic, restricted to a wheel chair. As a teenager she broke her neck in a diving accident and is unable to care for herself. She is constantly accompanied by her husband or staff.

Because I was sitting next to Joni that night I was asked if I would help feed her. That was a humbling experience for me, considering how much practice I've had! But for her it was a daily routine. As the evening flew by her handicap was overshadowed by her enthusiasm for life.

I was thinking to myself how easily Joni could have chosen to let one tragic event scar her self-esteem and spoil her outlook on life. But she chose a different course. We talked for about an hour and not once did I hear a word of complaint or "poor me" come from her lips. Instead, she turned her attention toward the needs and interests of others. At some point Joni made the decision to follow the principles I'm writing about in this chapter.

She didn't turn inward or pull away from life and people. She didn't focus only on the negative side of the coin but took the time and effort to turn it over and make something wonderful of the good that remained. She has accepted the past but chose not to be defined by it.

Since her accident, Joni has developed a ministry for handicapped people, has her own radio program, and continues to write, sing, and draw beautiful paintings with a brush between her teeth. She didn't deny her limitations—she learned how to accept the past for what it was and how it left her and chose to build on her strengths. And she has done well at that.

Joni's handicap is visible and therefore makes a clear illustration of the healing process. But for many of you the emotional handicap is not as easy to notice or make allowance for at first glance. Even so, you can work through the events and consequences of your disabling past and achieve a positive, productive outlook on life.

4. *Learn from your hurts.* We have the dumbest cat in the state of Arizona. This cat had the bad habit of pawing around in the laundry room and sleeping in the laundry basket. Day after day, Donna would shoo him away or put him outside. But every time the cat came back into the house he headed right for the laundry room to rub cat hair on our clothes.

Well, one day he made a serious mistake and was about to learn the lesson of his life. On this particular afternoon, the cat covered himself up with the warm, damp laundry waiting to be dried. So when Donna emptied the basket into the dryer she didn't notice that the cat went along for the ride. She closed the dryer door, pressed the "On" button and came into the living room where I was sitting reading a book.

Suddenly we heard the strangest sound coming from the laundry room—a "clunk, clunk . . . clunk, clunk" noise. It went on for a minute or so, and I finally asked Donna jokingly, "Does my underwear normally make that much noise in the dryer?" We realized something was in the machine that wasn't supposed to be, so we went to check.

When the door opened, out jumped a cat with a mission—to get out of the house as soon as possible. With his hair standing straight out as though he had just been charged with electricity, our cat took off. Before we could reach him to see if he was OK, he was out the back door, over the wall, and gone. We didn't see him for six hours. And then he only peeked in the patio door to see if things were safe.

The point is, the cat learned a valuable lesson that day—stay away from the laundry room. In fact, he now makes a point to go all the way around the house and come in the patio door in order to keep a safe distance from the clothes basket! That cat is not about to make the same mistake twice.

Like our cat, many of us have learned a great deal through painful experiences. The psalmist pictures this truth, saying, "Before I was afflicted I went astray, but now I obey your word" (Psalm 119:67). But unlike the cat, we shouldn't simply run away. Sometimes it's the difficult and traumatic experiences in life that teach us the greatest lessons.

Joyce's father memories were of a father who drank too much, offered little guidance, squandered the family income, and disciplined unfairly with no consistency. And he took every opportunity to criticize young Joyce. The impact was profound on Joyce as a child and later as she entered marriage. But as a result of a new and growing relationship with God, Joyce started to change. Her attitudes and thinking began to take on a healthier approach.

As we talked about her father memories and what she learned from them, she listed the following:

- Alcohol and life don't mix well.
- Responsible parenting requires responsible discipline.
- A budget can save a family from financial ruin.
- Love is more than a feeling.
- Criticism hurts people; encouragement builds them up.

Joyce learned those lessons a very hard way. She did not choose her family and was not responsible for the treatment she received. Even so, her father memories taught her much about life—especially about what not to do. Because she was determined not to put herself back in an abusive situation, Joyce refused to date anyone who was not a committed Christian with a history of responsible, kind, self-controlled behavior. Today she is happily married and providing a loving, stable home for her daughter. She has learned from her hurts.

Joyce chose to take control of her life and redirect it. Have you? Or when you think about your past, or even your present, do you feel more like that cat thumping around out of control in the dryer of life? If so, you may just be waiting for someone to come and open the door and let you out of your misery. The good news is, Christ has already come to set you free and to open the door that leads to health and wholeness.

Someone once wrote about his need for help this way:

The Pit

A man fell into a pit and couldn't get himself out.

A SUBJECTIVE person came along and said:
"I feel for you down there."

An OBJECTIVE person came along and said:
"It's logical that someone would fall down there."

A PHARISEE said:
"Only bad people fall into a pit."

A MATHEMATICIAN
calculated how he fell into the pit.

A NEWS REPORTER
wanted the exclusive story of his pit.

A FUNDAMENTALIST said:
"You deserve your pit."

An I.R.S. man
asked if he was paying taxes on his pit.

A SELF-PITYING person said:
"You haven't seen anything until you've seen MY PIT!"

A CHARISMATIC said:
"Just confess that you're not in a pit."

An OPTIMIST said:
"Things could be worse!"

A PESSIMIST said:
"Things will get worse!"

JESUS, seeing the man, took him by the hand and LIFTED
HIM OUT of the pit.

—Source Unknown[6]

The question is, are you ready to get out of the pain cycle, learn from the experience, and change your future behavior to avoid the situation from now on? With God's help you can.

DON'T LET YOUR FATHER MEMORIES DEFINE WHO YOU ARE

To begin acquiring a new identity and maturity in Christ, tear off the negative labels assigned to you in childhood.

"You're stupid." "You're shy." "You're pretty." "You're the bright one in the family." Those are the labels people get stuck with. From the time we were born, others have been trying to put labels on us. It begins with parents and other family members, and it continues with peers and society as we grow older.

We spend time teaching our children that "just because someone calls you something, that doesn't make it true." If I call a football a bat, that doesn't make it a bat. If someone calls you a dummy, that doesn't mean you are one. Don't let others stick on destructive labels! And be very careful about what you call yourself. Avoid labeling other people or situations in life.

Many times others didn't even mean to label us—it just happened. Perhaps it was the result of a physical characteristic or the role you assumed. It could also be a result of birth order, the color of your skin, or your ability or lack of ability. Can you think of any labels you wear? Maybe it's one of these:

- I'm the black sheep.
- I'm the good kid.

- I'm the peacemaker.
- I'm the rebellious one.
- I'm the listening ear.
- I'm the athletic one.
- I'm the stubborn one.
- I'm the family planner.
- I'm the quiet one.
- I'm the outsider.
- I'm the baby in the family.

Corrie ten Boom did not let the events of her life define who she became. Suffering through the violence of the holocaust didn't determine how she responded to life. She writes in her book, *In My Father's House*:

> For helping and hiding the Jews, my father, my brother's son and my sister all died in prison. My brother survived his imprisonment, but died soon afterward. Only Nollie, my older sister, and I came out alive.
>
> So many times we wonder why God has let certain things happen to us. We try to understand the circumstances of our lives, and we are left wondering. But God's foolishness is so much wiser than our wisdom.
>
> From generation to generation, from small beginnings and little lessons, He has a purpose for those who know and trust Him.
>
> God has no problems—just plans![7]

Take the events of your past, including your father memories, and ask yourself: "Am I allowing these events to define who I am today and influence my behavior?" If the definition you are operating from is healthy and good, that's great. If it's negative and self-defeating, it's time to make some changes and peel off some old labels.

Start by correcting your thinking and specific behaviors—let your emotions follow along at their own pace. The first step in changing your life is changing your mind. With God's help you can change your thinking patterns and begin to put the past in its rightful place.

NOTES

1. Michael Reagan with Joe Hyams, *Michael Reagan: On the Outside Looking In* (New York: Kensington, 1988), p. 7.
2. Ibid., p. 8.
3. Ibid., p. 15.
4. Ibid., p. 12.
5. Barbara Johnson, *Stick a Geranium in Your Hat and Be Happy* (Waco, Tex.: Word, 1990), p. 84.
6. Ibid., pp. 14-15.
7. Corrie ten Boom with C. C. Carlson, *In My Father's House* (Old Tappan, N.J.: Revell, 1976), p. 16.

13

JUST DO IT

You can take what you've learned about father memories and respond in one of two ways:

1. After you finish reading this book you can put it up on the shelf with the others and say, "That was interesting." And that's the end of that. It will never change your life.
2. Or you can take what you've learned and apply it to your life—and make some changes. It may be risky but it will bring growth, happiness, and healing.

I hope that you will process what you have read and let it have a lasting effect on your life. Exploring father memories can make a difference. What once was the state of your life and your family as a child does not have to determine what always will be the state of your life and your family today.

Mexican-American actor Edward James Olmos, who is best known for his role as the police chief on the television program "Miami Vice," grew up poor in East Los Angeles. His early memories were of far less than ideal circumstances—poverty, a dirt-floor kitchen, his parents' divorcing when he was just a child. Today Olmos has this to say to kids who think they don't have a future:

I tell them we're all given a choice. Some people say they didn't have a choice. They're poor or brown or crippled. They had no parents. Well, you can use any one of those excuses to keep your life from growing. Or you can say, "Okay, this is where I am, but I'm not going to let it stop me. Instead, I'm gonna turn it around and make it my strength."

That's what I did.[1]

Like Edward James Olmos, you can press on to become more than your memories dictate. Even if your memories are filled with pain, anger, abuse, confusion, or resentment, *you are not trapped.*

- You did survive.
- You made it.
- Your life is still ahead of you.
- God still has a plan for your today and tomorrow.

The question is: What now? What does God want me to do today?

THIS MOMENT TODAY

All of us are asked to overcome some disappointments in life because we live in a fallen world populated by imperfect people who cannot perfectly satisfy our needs. Regardless of how much Dad did right, there will be times he let us down. As psychologist Larry Crabb explains,

Many of us have wonderful parents, and I do, for whom we are deeply grateful. But all of us long for what the very best parent can never provide: perfect love. Love that's always there with understanding, deeply and sacrificially concerned at every moment for our welfare, never too burdened with its own cares to be sensitive to ours, strong enough to handle a full awareness of our faults without retreating, and wise enough to direct us properly at every crossroad. No parent measures up to those standards, yet our heart will settle for nothing less. And because every child naturally turns to this primary caregiver for what he desperately wants, every child is disappointed.[2]

Therefore, part of the process of becoming mature involves learning to accept that disappointment is both inevitable and surmountable. When you look at your father memories you may feel disappointed with yourself, your father, or your circumstances. But as an adult you can choose to learn from the past, to do things differently, and to dedicate yourself to the hope that will never disappoint—trusting in God. Although God and others want to help you mature in Christ, no one else can do it for you.

I started this book by picturing father memories as initials carved in the trunk of a tree. When I see my growing children, the mark I am leaving on their lives is becoming more clear to me. I wish I could change some things and make them new—but I can't. I can only ask my children's forgiveness and alter my actions today in the hope of correcting yesterday's mistakes. There are also some results of my fathering that I wouldn't change for the world—I'm rewarded for my efforts a hundredfold when I see biblical character qualities mirrored in my children.

I am now the father making memories for my children. And sooner than I'd like, I'll be taking my dad's place and my children will be taking mine. That's a scary thought to a forty-year-old man waiting for his midlife crisis to hit! I had little idea when I became a father thirteen years ago that so much would be riding on me as a daddy. And I didn't know then how quickly the years would pass.

Bill and Gloria Gaither wrote the song "We Have This Moment Today." In it they paint a beautiful word picture of how the moments of our lives pass like sand through our fingers. Over and over, we're confronted with little reminders that time is short. Life needs to be lived—not worried about, regretted, or merely endured. If there is anything from your past that is hurting or holding you back from doing what God intended for your life, it's time to break the cycle and live life as God wants—abundantly.

I permitted the cautiousness created by my own father memories and temperament to keep me from much of life's fullness. One day it dawned on me that I was holding back instead of jumping in, praying without pursuing, and looking without ever taking a leap—or just a solid step forward from my comfort zone.

But by specific choices and directed effort I've made large strides in the direction of breaking the cycle of cautiousness. I'm learning to practice what I preach—that cautiousness is *not* next to godliness. I'm not striving to become the spontaneous, fearless, sometimes reckless man King David was. I want to be the quietly courageous, spiritually bold, and confident man God created *me* to be.

Last night I was watching my children's teddy bear hamsters run like crazy on their exercise wheels. They were running as fast as they could make their little feet go, and yet they weren't getting anywhere. They always ended up in the same place—no ground gained.

Replaying hurtful memories over and over without taking action is similar to those furry rodents running in place. You end up emotionally exhausted, and time is used up in an unproductive cycle. But the same emotional power *could* be directed at achieving worthwhile goals in the process of personal and professional growth. You are brighter than the average teddy bear hamster. You can get off the treadmill of bondage and delusions of past thought patterns.

Stuck in the Muck?

If you put water and dirt together, what do you get? Mud. It is not a pretty sight. If you put a few negative father memories together with the stress of living these days, what do you get? Memory muck. Even the most intelligent, educated, loving adults can get stuck in the muck of life. Are there any muddy footprints from your past tracking up your home today? Put a check next to the behaviors you see in yourself:

_____ Depression
_____ Anger, bitterness
_____ Perfectionism, compulsiveness
_____ Procrastination
_____ Worry, fear
_____ Impulsiveness
_____ Controlling need to please others
_____ Overeating, smoking, substance abuse
_____ Abusing or neglecting others
_____ Workaholism

There is a lie or there are lies in your self-talk that leads you into these and other self-destructive behavior patterns. Throughout this book I have encouraged you to use the powerful tool of father memories to uncover those lies and discover healthier ways of handling life and relating to others. The exercises in this book are not intended to excuse your behavior—only to help explain and change it.

The focus is not on your father. It is where it should be—on you. You are responsible to stop the sin you find in your life. With God's help you can pass on a healthier heritage to your own children, giving them the gift of sweet and precious father memories.

BREAKING THE CYCLE

Change is possible. But only permanent change is worth the effort in the long run. Change that lasts for only a few days or weeks promises something it can't deliver. It's like spitting at a campfire—the intent is right but the results fall short.

If negative behavior is holding you hostage from happiness and fulfillment in relationships, then lasting change is necessary. You don't need to stay tied to the negative and unhealthy messages your father memories are whispering in your thought life.

Les Carter, in *Imperative People,* put it this way:

> Many imperative people remember problems in the past and assume that the future will bring more of the same. These people vow, *I will never let this happen again.* For example, a wife may recall the arguments, or perhaps physical abuse, from her childhood and vow, *We're not going to have such disagreements in our home.* She then expends tremendous energy trying to force harmony. . . . The mind is so obsessed with preventing old problems that satisfaction is not recognized in present situations. The imperative person is a prisoner of the past.[3]

Are you a prisoner of the past? Throughout this book we have talked about practical ways to break negative patterns of thinking and behavior. I've encouraged you to:

1. Use father memories to identify the lies underlying behavior.
2. Face the hurt—don't pull away.
3. Learn from the hurts of your past.

4. Don't let your father memories define who you are.
5. Replace the old script with new, healthy change beginning today.

FORGIVENESS AND FREEDOM

As I stated in an earlier chapter, Michael Reagan faced a life-long struggle of feeling as though he was "on the outside looking in." In his autobiography he talked about those feelings and his struggle to forgive. In the final analysis, he did the right thing—and he's enjoying inner freedom as a result of his choice.

In the last paragraph of his book, Michael pulled it all together. As you read what he wrote, I encourage you to make his words your own. "I realize now that all during my childhood I never told my parents that I loved them and never appreciated the love that they gave me," Michael says. "However, the most important thing I have learned from examining my life is that if we children are to survive we must first learn to forgive our parents, and hopefully our parents will also forgive us."[4]

Without forgiveness of others and ourselves, and obedience to God, it all comes apart. Peace turns to pieces. Rest turns to restlessness. And the joy of obedience is lost in a mire of sin.

TURN IT AROUND

Billy Graham's daughter Gigi Tchividjian turned her thought life and spiritual life around. She recalls an incident involving her famous father:

> I remember one clear, crisp day when we had been playing up behind our house. A large hollow stump, perched high above the road near a red clay bank, was our fort. We had stocked it with red clay balls (which, more than once, were tossed upon the unsuspecting cars below). On this particular day, I had been playing with friends and had been naughty—a fact that was causing my conscience to hurt badly. The more uncomfortable I became, the harder I played, trying desperately to ignore my conscience. I told myself that what I had done was really not so bad, and that, after all, no one would find out about it. But still I felt miserable.
>
> Suddenly I heard the sound of a car, then commotion in my driveway below. When I heard my daddy's voice, I froze. He had

arrived home unexpectedly early. How ashamed I was! I felt cold, then hot. Of all people, I longed to please him. What should I do?

I ran as fast as I could down the hill into the waiting, loving arms of my father, with the assurance that, even if he did find out about my wrongdoing, he would still love me and forgive me.[5]

Gigi tells us much about herself today in this little story. I caught that:

- she is a duty bound, positive pleaser.
- she struggles with not being perfect, and with wanting to be the good girl she thinks she is supposed to be.
- her intense desire to please indicates that she is a first class giver, whose middle name could be changed to "Service."
- she has a healthy view of men.
- she has a healthy trust in her father's unconditional love and willingness to forgive, which leads me to believe she would approach her heavenly Father with the same confidence today as an adult.

However, the big lie that Gigi struggled with in her life was this—"I must be perfect."

Gigi's own writings and life history confirm that her memory-related insights are right on target. "Try as I would, I could never measure up to all I thought the Lord wanted me to be, or all I thought I should be." Gigi goes on to say, "Some people just seem to have an easy time living the Christian life. Not me! And, after leaving his calling card of discouragement on the doorstep of my heart, Satan also convinced me that since I was not 'perfect' I certainly had no right to minister to others."[6]

The picture of a "calling card of discouragement" says it well. Every day someone is handing us that calling card. It could be the calling card of discouragement, or perfectionism, or anger, or depression, or a hundred other destructive behaviors or thinking patterns. Whatever the calling card is in your life, you can refuse to let the caller in.

As the old saying about sin and temptation relates, you can't keep a bird from lighting on your head, but you can keep him from building a nest in your hair. You may never stop ingrained, negative thoughts from popping into your mind, but you can discipline yourself to refute them with truth and shoo them away each and every time they show up.

Gigi didn't stay frozen in despair. As she had run as a child to her earthly father's arms, so now as an adult she ran to her heavenly Father and trusted in God's love. "Suddenly a beautiful realization dawned—*We don't have to be perfect to be a blessing.* We are asked only to be real, trusting in His perfection to cover our imperfection, knowing that one day we will finally be all that Christ saved us for and wants us to be."[7]

Gigi put her father memory to work for her. So can you. Gigi's story points out four keys to turning our lives around:

1. Get your life right with God.
2. Trust in your heavenly Father's love.
3. Give up the perfectionism, or whatever is holding you back.
4. Be real with yourself and others.

BUILD A NEW FOUNDATION

Trust in God and others is a key to change. Gigi knew that her daddy's arms were wide open. She had a great foundation of love and acceptance to build upon. But for some of you there are giant cracks in the concrete of your life. Your search for a stable foundation will never rest on your relationship with your father or your family of origin. In many cases, trusting an earthly father would be both impossible and inadvisable.

When I talked to June about trust she just laughed. "After all my old man put me through I not only don't trust him, I don't ever want to see him again," she said.

I wondered what kind of terrible things he could have done to prompt that kind of reaction. So I asked. June's story was typical of women from abusive families. However, she chose a different response than most.

June recalled a great deal of anger, abuse, and general confusion in her family. As the eldest daughter she received the brunt of her father's anger. He made clear that he was boss of everything and everybody in the family. June, being an independent child, chose to challenge his authority. What she got in return for rebellion was harshness, anger, and physical abuse. At age fourteen she checked out of the house and hit the streets.

Over the past eight years she continued to be abused by men, continuing the cycle. All she did was jump from the frying pan into the fire. And now at age twenty-two, her once pliable personality was hard, callous, and distrusting—especially of men. It seemed as though every man who had touched her life blasted away another piece of trust from her already flimsy foundation—and I knew she had her doubts about me. Rightfully so, considering all she had been through.

"Do you see how your relationship with your father has made trusting men difficult?" I asked. "It's even hard for you to trust me, isn't it?"

"Yes," June responded directly to the point.

"Do you ever want to trust men again?" I asked.

"Sure, if there was really someone who could live up to my trust. Which I doubt there is," she responded.

After weeks of counseling June is starting to cultivate appropriate levels of trust in relationships. She is making real progress because she is now convinced that without trust her life will always lack intimate friendships.

She is right. Building relationships without trust is like trying to nail Jello® to a tree—guaranteed frustration.

If your father memories have left you struggling with trust, here are six things June has been working on that will help you:

1. *Take small steps.* Don't expect too much too soon. Over many years trust was broken. It will take much time for trust to be reestablished.
2. *Learn whom to trust and whom not to trust.* Not everyone should be trusted. The degree that you can safely trust someone relates directly to the closeness and commitment in the relationship. Trust is built over time with those of proved character. It is better to have a few special people who have earned your trust than to naively assume that you can be vulnerable enough to trust everyone.
3. *Don't give up on trusting special friends just because one individual lets you down.* Jesus didn't stop trusting John because of Judas. People who have been hurt tend to

lump everybody in the same foul batch of dough. Their peculiar and understandable logic goes like this: If my father can't be trusted, then men can't be trusted. Beware of destructive generalizations.

4. *Don't be afraid to confront.* Trust your judgment to confront another person if needed. If you have reason to question someone's actions, speech, or behavior toward you, lovingly confront him. Get it all out in the open and don't be intimidated. If you have been hurt, tell those who hurt you. Set boundaries; don't be used. Get others to back you up if necessary.

5. *Don't put your trust in the wrong things.* Those who can't trust people tend to trust things. That's a mistake. The Scripture says, "The rich man thinks of his wealth as an impregnable defense, a high wall of safety. What a dreamer!" (Proverbs 18:11, TLB). Possessions and financial security will fail to meet your inner needs.

6. *Trusting God is always safe.* God is the author of trust. He is trustworthy. Unlike people, who will knowingly and unknowingly hurt us, God's intentions are pure and kind. Trusting God is a firm foundation for life. Isaiah wrote, "Trust in the Lord forever, for the Lord, the Lord, is the Rock eternal" (Isaiah 26:4). Make sure you know Him personally as your Lord and Savior.

June is changing. She is breaking the cycle from her father memories, telling herself the truth. She is working hard to walk a new path hand in hand with the heavenly Father, who loves her tenderly. She has been able to let loose of the hurt and pain from her childhood to grab hold of the future. She is confronting those who hurt her and treating herself and others with proper respect.

Father memories are not the end of the story. You write the script for a happy ending—not your dad. If you die with angry, hurtful, or bitter words on your lips or in your mind that will be because you let them live there.

It is your responsibility to start the process of change. It is God's part to bless that decision and empower you.

It's Over Before You Know It

Fathers usually die before their children. Perhaps your father is already gone. Simple math tells us that our fathers will not be here for the rest of our lives. But your father memories will. So it's time to do something positive with the memories you have to work with.

As the Nike advertisement tells us: *Just do it!*

Yesterday I was standing next to my dad as he lay in the intensive care unit of the hospital. My mother and I had stood at his bedside before, each time wondering if he had the strength to recover from another surgery. Serious health problems have brought my father near death many times over the past few years.

Watching my dad labor to live has done something to me. It's helped me to grow up. It's made me more aware of what's really important in life. I'm discovering that the little disagreements, and even the big ones, the hurts, the collecting of stuff, book deadlines, radio programs, speaking engagements, and the spotlights of life aren't so important. Today may be the only day Dad and I have left to express our love for one another. I want to make positive father memories, not only for us to share but also to share with my children.

Life is to be experienced, enjoyed, wrestled with, and ultimately accepted for what it is—a series of events designed to knock off the rough edges and conform us more completely to the image of our Creator. Your father memories, and mine, have a place in that process. Yet, ultimately, it is God who can cause all things to work together for our good,[8] and He promises to do so. Regardless of our past, our future is bright with hope as we trust our heavenly Father.

Notes

1. From the excerpt "A Matter of Choice," by Tom Seligson, in *Parade*, as quoted in *Reader's Digest*, "Personal Glimpses," November 1991, p. 54.
2. Larry Crabb, *Inside Out* (Colorado Springs: NavPress, 1988), p. 107.
3. Les Carter, *Imperative People* (Nashville: Thomas Nelson, 1991), p. 52.

4. Michael Reagan with Joe Hyams, *Michael Reagan: On the Outside Looking In* (New York: Kensington, 1988), p. 286.
5. Gigi Graham Tchividjian, *Weather of the Heart* (Portland, Oreg.: Multnomah, 1991), p. 166.
6. Ibid., p. 61.
7. Ibid., p. 62.
8. See Romans 8:28.

EPILOGUE

My mother called this past week and recounted some moving experiences that had come to mind as she considered her own father memories. She recalled that on her fourteenth birthday, her dad wrote in her autograph book words that reflected his character and love for his family. She still cherishes the inscription he wrote: "A good name is rather to be chosen than great riches, and loving favour rather than silver and gold" (Proverbs 22:1, KJV*).

Her voice cracked with emotion as she read aloud the poem she had recently written expressing her appreciation of her dad. Although her dad has been dead for forty years, his legacy of love lives on. The character traits and values of my grandfather—integrity, a good sense of humor, respect from and toward others—have been passed down through the generations.

Tears came to my eyes as I considered how much my life, and my children's lives, have been enriched by my grandfather's faithfulness as a father years ago, even though I never knew him. He died when my mother was only sixteen.

I asked Mom if I could use her poem to close this book, as a fitting tribute to fathers everywhere. I hope it is an encouragement and a challenge to you. Even if it doesn't ring true for your dad, it certainly fits our Father in heaven.

* King James Version.

Dad

Dad, you gave me life,
    The family name to hold.
    You taught me humble pride,
    And purity, fine as gold.

Dad, you gave me love.
    You always held my hand.
    You gave me trusting faith,
    That in hard times will stand.

Dad, you gave me strength.
    You showed me how to smile.
    You were my constant friend,
    Down many a weary mile.

Dad, you gave me guidance,
    To always choose the right.
    To help a needy neighbor,
    Even in the cold of night.

Dad, you gave to me a goal,
    To follow all my dreams,
    And gave me loving praise;
    Today, how much it means.

Dad, you are my tower;
    You hold a special place.
    When walking in your footsteps,
    There I see your noble face.

Dad, you were a Godly man;
    You taught me how to pray,
    To love the Lord forever;
    His Word will light the way.

Dad, many years have passed away
    Since you said "good-bye" to me.
    I'll look for you in Heaven,
    Where we'll spend eternity!

Randy L. Carlson is available for seminars
on the topics of

> Early Memories
> Father Memories
> Marriage
> Parenting
> The Family in the Family Business

To find out more about having Randy Carlson
bring one of his seminars to your church or group,
please write or call:

> Randy L. Carlson
> P.O. Box 37,000
> Tucson, AZ 85740
> (602) 742-6976

Moody Press, a ministry of the Moody Bible Institute,
is designed for education, evangelization, and edification.
If we may assist you in knowing more about Christ
and the Christian life, please write us without obligation:
Moody Press, c/o MLM, Chicago, Illinois 60610.